Call Me Diana

THE PRINCESS OF WALES
ON HERSELF

Nigel Cawthorne

GIBSON SQUARE

This edition first published in the UK in 2016 by Gibson Square

info@gibsonsquare.com

www.gibsonsquare.com

Tel: +44 (0)20 7096 1100 (UK)

Tel: +1 646 216 9813 (USA)

ISBN   9781783340125

Contents

Introduction

Twenty years after she died, it was decided to erect a statue of Diana, Princess of Wales in the grounds of Kensington Palace, her former home. It is to be paid for by William and Harry, from money they receive from the Duchy of Cornwall, and private fundraising. One cannot imagine that it would be undersubscribed. More than two decades after her tragic death, Diana is still the "people's princess" – a title co-opted by Tony Blair during the national outpouring of grief in 1997 – and – what she always wanted to be – the "queen of people's hearts".

During a life lived in the glare of publicity, Diana blossomed from being a shy, awkward, teenage, nursery teacher's assistant to the ultimate fashion icon, said to be the most photographed woman in the world. She was also known worldwide for her compassion for the sick, dying and disadvantaged. And this was not just for public consumption. When she visited hospitals, hospices or hovels, she often asked her minders to stay outside so she could have a private chat with victims.

At a meeting in Rome in 1992, Mother Teresa told her: "To heal other people you have to suffer yourself."

Diana nodded vigorously in agreement.

It is clear that she had, indeed, suffered. She admitted being unfaithful to Prince Charles with James Hewitt. This was a sensational thing to have done. It, technically, put her lover's life in jeopardy. Under the 1381 Treason Act it was declared high treason to have sex with the wife of the heir to the throne. Treason was still punishable by death and the death penalty itself was only outlawed in 1998. But Diana was held in such high regard and thought to have been treated so abominably that no-one could begrudge her a moment of happiness.

Since her death millions of words have been written about Diana. But looking back from this distance it is her own words that have an enduring importance. Various *bon mots* from Morton's book and Bashir's interview have achieved wide circulation. Numerous asides were recorded by journalists. Other quotes on the internet are more difficult to source, perhaps taken from private conversations. Some have the ring of authenticity about them. Others are more dubious and find no place within these pages.

Here I have attempted to present the distilled essence of the person the whole world took to their hearts – except, perhaps, those in Buckingham Palace she effortlessly upstaged with her innocence, charm and grace.

Still, she was missed in all quarters. A memorial service for the 185 people who died in the earthquake in Christchurch, New Zealand, in 2011 William said:

"My grandmother once said that grief is the price we pay for love."

The Queen herself said: "No one who knew Diana will ever forget her."

Marking Diana's passing Mother Teresa, who herself died at the age of eighty-seven on the eve of Diana's funeral, said: "She helped me to help the poor. That's the most beautiful thing."

Father Frank Gelli, the former curate of St Mary Abbots Church, Kensington, who conducted an annual remembrance service in front of the palace gates, said: "Princess Diana was a wonderful, caring philanthropist. She would come sometimes into the church and sit at the back and pray."

Harry spoke for everyone when he told the *People*: "When she died, there was a gaping hole, not just for us but also for a huge amount of people across the world. If I can try and fill a very small part of that, then job done. I will have to, in a good way, spend the rest of my life trying to fill that void as much as possible. And so will William."

William, himself, added: "Over the years, I personally feel as though my mother has been there, she's always there." Many people share that feeling.

At her funeral in Westminster Abbey her brother, Earl Spencer drew attention to the fact that, all over the world, she was a symbol of selfless humanity, a standard-bearer for the rights of the truly downtrodden, a very British girl who transcended nationality.

She was someone with a natural nobility who was

classless, he said: "She needed no royal title to continue to generate her particular brand of magic."

The couturier Oscar de la Renta, whose elegant gowns she often showed off, concurred, pointing out: "Diana had a natural sense of royalty that no royalty can match."

And she knew how to wear a dress to good effect. On the evening Charles was confessing to adultery with Camilla Parker Bowles, Diana had an invitation to the Serpentine Gallery's summer party. She wore a figure-hugging black silk number, by Greek designer Christina Stambolian, which became known as the "revenge dress".

"'She thought it was too daring," said Stambolian, until Diana changed her mind at the last minute. She looked a drop-down gorgeous and everybody realised that that dress was making a bold statement.

But Diana's look transcended her clothes. "I think every decade has an iconic blonde, like Marilyn Monroe or Princess Diana and, right now, I'm that icon," said Paris Hilton in 2006. However, apart from one incident in 1994 when a paparazzo snapped a picture of Diana sunbathing topless, she was not known for conspicuous nudity or, indeed, pornographic videos. Or as one internet meme put it: "In a world full of Kardashians, be Diana."

Diana was so famous that even God, or at least his voice in Hollywood Morgan Freeman, craved an audience.

"Which lady would I like to meet?" he is quoted as

saying. "Um, I don't know that there's anybody left that I didn't meet. But the one that I really wanted to meet died and that was Princess Diana. I really wanted to get to know her. I like her."

Then there is Donald Trump, United States President.

"I only have one regret in the women department," he wrote in *The Art of the Comeback*. "I never had the opportunity to court Lady Diana Spencer."

In November 1997, three months after Princess Diana had died, NBC's Stone Phillips asked him: "Do you think you would have seriously had a shot?"

"I think so, yeah," Trump replied. "I always have a shot."

Another womanising US president had a more measured view. On news of Diana's death Bill Clinton said: "Hillary and I admired her for her work for children, for people with AIDS, for the cause of ending the scourge of land mines in the world and for her love for her children William and Harry."

Israeli Prime Minister Benjamin Netanyahu said: "She represented Britain with nobility and warmth and she captured the imagination of millions throughout the world with her dedication to her children and to innumerable worthy causes. Her untimely death is a shock to all who admired her and who will cherish her memory."

Nelson Mandela was also full of praise. They had met when Diana visited South Africa in 1997. Six years later, when announcing that the Nelson Mandela

Children's Fund was planning to join the Diana, Princess of Wales Memorial Fund to help South Africans with HIV/AIDS and their families, and to assist children orphaned by the disease, he told a press conference in London: "Caring for people who are dying and helping the bereaved was something for which Diana had passion and commitment. When she stroked the limbs of someone with leprosy, or sat on the bed of a man with HIV/AIDS and held his hand, she transformed public attitudes and improved the life chances of such people. People felt if a British princess can go to a ward with HIV patients, then there's nothing to be superstitious about."

Afterwards Mandela visited Althorp and put a wreath on her grave.

Those who knew her also commented on her sense of humour. Sarah, Duchess of York, said: "She had the best wit of anybody."

It was perhaps not without a hint of irony that one of her favourite phrases was: "The things I do for England."

"Diana loved to giggle. She loved to laugh. We had many, many wonderful times together," said Elton John. "She was fun and accessible, that's why people loved her."

His reworking of the song "Candle in the Wind" as a tribute has swelled the coffers of Diana's charities with its global takings.

George Michael said: "We clicked in an intangible way, probably because of our upbringing." However, it is difficult to draw many parallels between the early lives of the son of a Cypriot restaurateur in North London and the daughter of an earl with a country estate.

She was, of course, the darling of other celebs.

"Only in storybooks do you get to dance with a princess until midnight. But it happened to me," said John Travolta after taking to the dance floor with Diana at the White House in 1985.

Nevertheless she remained resolutely down to earth. Cliff Richard tells the tale that, after dinner at a friend's house, Diana asked: "Do you have a pair of Marigolds?' I'll do the washing up." The host eventually convinced her there was no need.

The tributes have all be delivered. Now it is time to hear from Diana herself.

Call Me Diana

Diana on Diana

Princess Diana's most commonly quoted maxim was: "Carry out a random act of kindness, with no expectation of reward, safe in the knowledge that one day someone might do the same for you." It adorns a hundred posters and seems to have had its origin in the 1993 children's book *Random Kindness and Senseless Acts of Beauty*. But Diana made something more of it. The full quote was: "Perhaps we're too embarrassed to change or too frightened of the consequences of showing that we really care. But why not risk it anyway? Begin today. Carry out a random act of seemingly senseless kindness, with no expectation of reward or punishment, safe in the knowledge that one day, someone somewhere might do the same for you."

In the world of royalty that is hedged round with protocols and precedent, Diana was conscientiously unconventional. "I do things differently, because I don't go by a rule book," she said in 1995, "because I lead from the heart, not the head, and albeit that's got me into trouble in my work, I understand that. But someone's got to go out there and love people and show it."

"It is a weakness that I lead from my heart, and not my head?"

She also said: "I like to be a free spirit. Some don't like that, but that's the way I am." But, as her marriage crumbled, she was more assertive, saying: "I am a free spirit – unfortunately for some."

"Each time one enjoys oneself – albeit it's in a different situation – you have to pay for it, because people criticise, which comes with the patch."

Once she had divorced and was stripped of her royal status, she grew ever more independent, telling a French newspaper: "No one can dictate my behaviour. I work by instinct, it's my best adviser. I touch people. I think that everyone needs that, whatever their age."

Diana was widely quoted as saying: "I have a woman's instinct and it's always a good one."

She claimed that was how she knew that Charles was continuing his relationship with Camilla, even though they were both married, and that he loved someone else.

"Oh, a woman's instinct is a very good one," she said. "I wasn't in a position to do anything about it.

But it wasn't all heartache. She told friends: "Everyone said I was the Marilyn Monroe of the 1980s and I was adoring every minute of it. Actually I've never sat down and said: 'Hooray, how wonderful. Never.' The day I do we're in trouble. I am performing a duty as the Princess of Wales as long as my time is allocated but I don't see it any longer than fifteen years."

Curiously her marriage to the Prince of Wales last almost exactly fifteen years, though she remained Diana, Princess of Wales for another year before her death. Marilyn Monroe's film career lasted just fifteen years too.

Diana admitted to being a technophobe. In 1984, she told the *Daily Mail*: "I don't even know how to use a parking meter, let alone a phone box."

The comment came after millionaire art dealer Oliver Hoare, who was friend of Charles and Diana, complained of a number of nuisance calls. These, apparently, emanated from the Princess's private line at Kensington Palace, her mobile telephone, and the home of her sister, Lady Sarah McCorquodale. Others were made in telephone boxes near the palace. The caller fell silent each time Mr Hoare answered.

"You cannot be serious," said Diana. "What have I done to deserve this? I feel I am being destroyed. There is absolutely no truth in it."

She told the newspaper that sinister forces were trying not only to harm her, but to undermine the monarchy. Hoare withdrew the complaint.

Diana wore her fame lightly. "It took a long time to understand why people were so interested in me," she said, "but I assumed it was because my husband had done a lot of wonderful work leading up to our marriage and our relationship."

The problem was that Diana soon outshone Charles, who was seen as being stuffy and out of touch.

Diana got to know herself and realised the talents she brought to the role.

"I've got tremendous knowledge about people and how to communicate," she said. "I've learnt that. I've got it. And I want to use it

But she did not rule out an element of luck.

"I'm lucky enough in the fact that I have found my role, and I'm very conscious of it, and I love being with people," she added.

The press paid little attention to Diana's religious beliefs, but in 1993 she had long discussions about religion and spirituality with the Reverend Tony Lloyd, Executive Director of the Leprosy Mission. She expressed an interest in conventional religions as well as astrology and psychic guidance, though Lloyd believed she was simply seeking after the truth.

Largely she kept her interest in New Age ideas to herself though.

"I'd never discuss it with anyone they would all think I was a nut. I used the word 'psychic' to my policemen a couple of times and they have freaked out."

However, she discussed the concept of heaven and life after death with Tony Lloyd.

"I find that fascinating and enticing," she said.

The Leprosy Mission, with its link to Mother Teresa, was one of the six charities she kept on after her divorce. The others were the Centrepoint charity, which provides shelter for the homeless, the English National Ballet, the National Aids Trust, Great Ormond Street Hospital for Sick Children, and the Royal Marsden Hospital in London, which specialises in cancer research and treatment.

Among the hundreds she gave up were the British Red Cross, Help the Aged, the Parkinson's Disease Society, Barnardo's and Relate. Charity consultant Fiona Fountain said the Princess' resignation likely cost charities a lot of financial support: "You can increase the price of a ticket so much more if you have got the Princess of Wales attending – it can add at least £50 to a ball ticket. That adds up."

John Mayo, director of Help the Aged, said their income had quadrupled under the Princess' patronage and they were "greatly saddened" to lose her.

"The Princess of Wales has brought light and hope to the lives of thousands of older people both at home and abroad," he said.

A few days before Diana announcement that she was retiring from public life, she told a reformed drug addict: "Learning to like yourself is the hardest thing everyone has to come to terms with their problems."

Although Diana was known and recognised around the

world, she said: "I actually don't like being the centre of attention."

She told her sister Jane: "I just love to get home and kick off my shoes, take off my smart clothes, get into jeans and a sweater. Then I really feel like myself, the real me."

Once free of her marriage, Diana asserted: "I have learned much over the last year. From now on I am going to own myself and be true to myself. I no longer want to live someone else's idea of what and who I should be. I am going to be me."

She told friends: "Inside the system I was treated very differently, as though I was an oddball and I felt I was an oddball, and so I thought I wasn't good enough. But now I think it's good to be the oddball, thank God.... Now, thank God, I think it's okay to be different."

Diana defended her shows of emotion and affection with the public in the face of criticism from some quarters.

"That's why I annoy certain people. Because I'm closer to people below me than to the people above me and the people above me don't forgive me for it," she said.

Despite the tribulations of her later years, she recalled an idyllic early childhood.

"A lot of nice things happened to me when I was in

nappies," she said.

Until 1975 when the family moved to Althorp, the Spencer family seat, Diana lived in Park House on the Queen's Sandringham Estate. It was her favourite childhood home.

"Endlessly explorable and filled with wonderful memories of so many pranks," she said. "I can see myself now seated on the nursery floor, playing with my toys, totally into my own thing."

And outside there was the estate to play in.

"I hated to be indoors," she said.

A sense of destiny came to her at an early age.

"I always felt very detached from everyone else," she said. "I knew I was going somewhere difference, that I was in the wrong shell."

That was, perhaps, because from birth she was a disappointment to her parents.

"I was supposed to be a boy," she said.

She had two older sisters, Sarah and Jane. Her younger brother Charles came along three years after her.

At West Heath private school in Sevenoaks, Kent, where she boarded from 1972 to 1977, she turned out to be something of a tomboy.

"I was a St. Trinian's-style terror, often in trouble," she admitted. "In spite of what my head teachers thought, I did actually learn something, although you wouldn't have known so from my O-level results. My years at West Heath were certainly happy ones. I made many friends, who I often see. Perhaps now when future generations are handing out punishments for talking after lights out, pillow fights, or illegal food, they will be told to run six times round this hall."

The other punishment, weeding the garden.

"I became a great expert at weeding," she said.

Otherwise: "I wasn't any good at anything at school; I just felt hopeless. A dropout."

Caring

When it came to the sick and vulnerable, Diana said: "I'd like people to think of me as someone who cares about them."

And they were not wrong.

"I am all about caring," she said. "I have always been like that."

She was also ready to reach out to those others shunned.

"For many people in our society, the idea of talking with someone who has been in care, whether it be a juvenile offender, a person who has suffered from mental illness or perhaps someone with learning difficulties is too awful to contemplate," she said. "I can assure them, it's not so bad! Not one of those I've met ever hurt me, was rude to me or treated me as though I was mad!"

She learnt early on to be forthright. After spending an hour in an overcrowded Women's Aid hostel for battered wives and children in Luton, Bedfordshire, in 1986, she told local housing chiefs: "They need another hostel."

Diana was an advocate of "care in the community" – the policy of tending for those suffering from mental illness outside outdated Victorian asylums put into action by Margaret Thatcher's Mental Health Act of 1983.

"We now recognise that many of those who were put into long-stay institutions need never have been put there in the first place," Diana said.

She had first-hand knowledge of this.

"One woman I vividly remember meeting had been 'put away' thirty years ago, suffering from post-natal psychosis, after the birth of her first child," she said. "Yet if the right support and resources had been available to her, she could so easily have continued to live in the community. Continued to enjoy what we all take for granted. Being able to go to bed when she was tired, not when the shift changed. Eating what she wanted, rather than being given food which offended the fewest taste buds. Being able to be private when she needed to, rather than having to share a room with four other people. No space, no privacy, no life!"

What's more the policy was working.

"Care in the community has made all the difference to this woman's life. She is now being helped to return to the community she left so long ago. Living in a homely environment with a small number of others, she is relearning the skills which had been lost to her. Savouring again the delights of a life she could barely remember."

In the care of the mentally ill, women had a special role Diana thought. "Each person is born with very individual qualities and potential," she said. "We as a society owe it to women to create a truly supportive environment in which they too can grow and move forward."

After all, she said: "Everyone has the potential to give something back."

There were dangers though. In a speech given by Princess Diana called "Does the Community Care?" on 17 November 1993, she said: "Recently a great deal of publicity has been given to a tiny number of people who have damaged themselves or others when they returned to the community from hospital care. It has raised very real concerns in many people. It's true there is a small minority who are rightly seen as a potential danger to the community who need greater levels of care and understanding. But however terrible these tragic cases are, they cannot be used as a way of dismissing the needs of thousands of others who are no threat to the community whatsoever."

Diana could even be quite political in her advocacy of care in the community.

"Finding the right kind of care in the community for each individual can never be seen as the soft option. Nor is it cheap," she said. "It requires the specialist skills of many different experts and organisations. A partnership, between doctors, health and local authorities, the voluntary and private sector and the police, all working together. Sharing their resources and undeniable talents to create an environment in which a person can develop and grow. But it's also a partnership between these dedicated carers and the person being cared for."

"Care in the community is a partnership. A partnership between skilled and caring professionals and a concerned and caring community. Working together, to find new ways of helping these people who've been excluded and connecting them with neighbours who will understand and accept them. By providing, proper funding for the homes they will need and the support they so rightly deserve, we can show them how much we care."

"Being asked to help decide what is best for themselves can leave the individual overwhelmed and frightened," she said. "Building on the work of 'Citizen Advocates', who defend the rights of people with learning difficulties, perhaps we could also learn from the help being given to people with AIDS."

While caring for all she met during here charity work, there was plainly something fragile about Diana. She needed caring too.

"Deep within us all is a need to care and to be cared for," she said. "We all have that right. Yet many people, in their attempt to build a life for themselves, lose touch with their own sense of belonging, of being part of something greater than themselves. They no longer believe they have the time or energy to give back to the community they live in, by helping those around them to build a happier life. Yet a community can only develop when individuals remember how dependant we all are on one another and reach out to those around them. Yet we continue to hear how people who live in the same street don't even acknowledge their neighbour's existence, let alone stop to say hello!"

It was a sensation she shared. "It's just by living at Kensington Palace – obviously it is a little bit isolating, but, you know, maybe we all feel like that."

In her public pronouncements, she seemed to make a covet appeal for care.

"Every single one of us needs to show how much we care for our community," she said, "care for each other and, in the process, care for ourselves."

Diana possessed a natural empathy. "I understand people's suffering, people's pain, more than you will ever know yourself," she said.

And she was determined to pass on that quality to her sons.

"I want my boys to have an understanding of people's emotions, their insecurities, people's distress, and their hopes and dreams," she insisted.

She wanted to do that for the whole country too. "I think the British people need someone in public life to give affection, to make them feel important, to give them light in their dark tunnels," she said using a chillingly prescient image. "I see it as a possibly unique role."

In her last interview in *Le Monde*, she said: "It all comes down to sincerity. You can't do anything good that you don't feel in your heart."

Throughout her busy and troubled life, Diana sought for one thing. "I've got to have a place where I can find peace of mind," she said. It was something she sought to give others in her hospital and hospice visits.

Visiting Poole General Hospital in 1988, Diana confided in a five-year-old girl recovering from a serious infection: "I take my teddy to bed every night and he travels with me everywhere I go" – thereby establishing an instant rapport with the child.

In New York in 1990, Diana visit a children's home for AIDS sufferers, where a three-year-old known as "Little Lady" asked if she could go for a drive.

"Of course you can come for a drive in my car," said Diana. Then she picked up the child and carried her to the limousine.

In 1996, Diana was visiting St Mary's Hospital in Paddington when the mother of a patient approached her. The woman's eleven-year-old daughter was seriously ill with pneumonia and had just come out of a coma. Diana went immediately to see the child and told her: "You are going to well again – you have youth on your side."

The girl had been expected to stay in hospital for at least eight weeks. After Diana's visit she was discharged after three days.

"It was a miracle," said the mother.

In 1995, Diana was given the Humanitarian of the Year award in New York. She said she was humbled by the honour, which she wished to share with parents, nurses, doctors and charity workers throughout the world.

"There are two basic ingredients that define us as human beings sharpness of mind and kindness of heart – hearing and sharing the grief of others," she said in her acceptance speech. "Today is the day of compassion. Let's not wait to be prompted. Let us demonstrate our humanity now."

Elsewhere in her speech she quoted Ella Wheeler Wilcox, a prolific turn-of-the-century American poet best known for her lines: "Laugh and the world laughs with you; Weep, and you weep alone." But Diana picked the short poem "The World's Need" for her acceptance speech, a four-line verse which says:

So many Gods, so many creeds,
So many paths that wind and wind,
While just the art of being kind
Is all the sad world needs.

At the same time Diana was extending her compassion to the whole world, *The Times* noted "her estranged husband burst on to the Internet with a speech about business and the environment".

Diana travelled the world and grew increasingly critical of the ethos of the West.

"In developed countries there is an increasing ethic of trying to grab so much for ourselves that we pretend we don't need each other," she said. "This, I have to say, is a dangerous myth. We should learn not how to survive each other but how to enjoy each other!"

When Prime Minister John Major had announced the "amicable separation" of the royal couple in December 1992, Labour MP Dennis Skinner, a long-time critic of the royal family, said: "We could now be witnessing the end of the monarchy."

But Diana was defiant. She told representatives of forty-two of her charities at a public conference in London: "Your patron has never been happier to see you. Whatever uncertainties the last few weeks may have brought, I want you to be certain of this: Our work together will continue unchanged. Especially at Christmas. The sick, the old, the handicapped and the homeless, the lonely, the confused and the simply unloved who are needing your help more than ever."

She was determined: "It's business as usual. I shall continue to carry on doing it my way."

In 1993, it was decided that Diana should cut down on her charity work. Announcing her withdrawal from public life, she offered her heartfelt thanks.

"To the wider public, may I say that I have made many friends. I have been allowed to share your thoughts and dreams, your disappointments and your happiness. You also gave me an education by teaching me more about life and living than any books or teachers could have done. My debt of gratitude to you all is immense. I hope, in some way, I have been of service in return. Your kindness and affection have carried me through some of the most difficult periods, and always your love and care have eased that journey. And for that, I thank you from the bottom of my heart. "

When a nineteen-year-old man with AIDS told her "You're more gorgeous than in the papers", she replied: "You should see me in the mornings."

Diana often brought humour to the task. Meeting a nervous, elderly man with one arm at Help the Aged home in 1986, she said: "I'll bet you have some fun chasing the soap around the bath."

That broke the ice. They then laughed and joked. He later described her as "gorgeous".

Shaking hands with an AIDS patient who was having a blood transfusion in 1988, Diana said: "Don't get up. You can't get away, anyway. You seem very attached! You are very brave. I'm very bad with needles. It makes me feel dizzy just looking at you."

Diana lightened the mood when visiting a Terrence Higgins Trust at an AIDS project in 1989. Casting aside all protocol, she took a stone out of her shoe and handed it to an official, saying: "I think this belongs to you."

Visiting a forty-six-year-old man suffering from AIDS at the Mortimer Market Centre, London, on 1 December 1994 – World AIDS Day, tension vanished when she quipped: "Your tie and shirt don't match."

He replied: "You should see my socks."

After the visit he said: "The encouragement she gives to people is outstanding."

When a brain scanner broke down at the National Hospital for Nervous Diseases she was visiting, Diana made light of the moment, saying: "Machines always seem to go wrong when I'm around."

She then comforted the waiting patient, saying: "Poor you."

Speaking at Help the Aged's Silver Jubilee reception in 1986, Diana said: "Growing old is, sadly, not always fun. There are elderly people in this country who fear for their financial and physical security. Many are concerned about their health, many are frail and worried about living an independent life." This demonstrated remarkable empathy for a twenty-five-year-old.

"It is tragic that elderly people cannot afford high electric and fuel bills," Diana said to a disabled pensioner at a Help the Aged day centre in 1986. The woman had told her that she often went to bed to escape the cold and Diana replied: "I suppose that's the best place to keep warm."

Later; the woman said, "Diana really does care for the elderly. She is an inspiration to us. "

Visiting Lodgemoor Hospital in Sheffield in 1994, a thirty-two-year-old paraplegic apologised from the unpleasant aroma of liniment applied during his physiotherapy. The quick-witted princess replied: "Don't worry, I can't smell it because I had a Chinese meal last night."

Diana was patron of Chickenshed, a theatre company which welcomes young people of all abilities. One of the members was a twenty-seven-year-old woman who suffered from cerebral palsy. Diana wrote her a letter, saying: "I hope you will always be able to let others share in your own strength."

She also wrote the foreword to her book *Paula's Story*. In it she said: "There is a saying: 'If a child lives with encouragement, he learns confidence. If a child lives with acceptance and friendship he learns to give love to the world.'"

Addressing the Federation of Small Businesses who

organised the Paralympic Games at Stoke Mandeville in 1984, Diana said: "How incredible it is that people with these disabilities can carry on as normal and get on with their lives."

Just a few days before she died, Diana told *Le Monde*: "I pay great attention to people and I always remember them. Every visit, every meeting is special. Nothing brings me more happiness than trying to help the most vulnerable people in society. It is a goal and essential part of my life, a kind of destiny. Whoever is in distress can call on me. I will come running, wherever they are."

Diana showed a particular empathy for people from minority groups. Expressing commiseration to the president of an association for Asian women whose community centre had been vandalised in 1991, she said: "It is very sad that you are facing a lot of problems… changing people's attitudes is a slow process.

At Tongagara refugee camp on the Zimbabwe-Mozambique border in 1993, Diana found a very sick woman lying on the ground. She crouched down and held the gnarled hands of the woman, who was suffering badly with leprosy.

"We must always leave them with hope," she said. "That's the most important thing.

Diana rescued a tramp who had fallen in the Regent's Canal by raising the alarm. Later she visited him in hospital and said: "You look much better than when I last saw you. I'll see you again at the weekend. God bless you."

She gave him some money and get-well-soon card.

"The lady's a miracle to me," he said.

Diana had managed to elude the paparazzi during the visit.

"Today of all days it meant a great deal to me not to be photographed," she said.

Nevertheless, the next day the newspapers carried full accounts of how Diana had saved the tramp.

Caring, for Diana, was a two-way street. She told Headway, the brain injury association: "In the past twelve years, I can honestly say, that one of my greatest pleasures has been my association with people like yourselves. During those years I have met many thousands of wonderful and extraordinary people, both here and around the world. The cared for and the carers."

After nursing her close friend Adrian Ward-Jackson, who died of AIDS, she wrote to their mutual friend Angela Serota, saying: "I reached a depth inside which I never imagined was possible. My outlook on life has changed its course and become more positive and balanced."

After that she no longer felt that she had to hide her true feelings behind a mask.

Asked if meeting dying people drained her, she replied: "No, never. When you discover you can give joy to people like that, there is nothing quite like it. William has begun to understand that too and I am hoping it will grow in him."

Nine months before she died, biographer Anthony Holden asked her what kind of man would tempt her to remarry. She replied: "Someone who understands what I'm about."

This gave him the opportunity to ask: "So what are you about?"

"I'm about caring, "she said. "I always have been, and I always will be. I thought I had married one caring man, but alas it didn't work out. Perhaps one day I will meet another."

Marriage

Asked by the press when he had first noticed Diana, Charles recalled she had been "an attractive sixteen-year-old". Her response was: "I suppose it makes a nice little segment of history, but I think he barely noticed me at all."

They met again three years later when she was nineteen.

"No more puppy fat," he remarked.

"I'm just taller now," she said, blushing. "I've stretched the puppy fat."

The encounter was at the estate of a mutual friend in the summer of 1980, shortly after the funeral of Charles' great uncle and mentor Lord Mountbatten which she had watched on television.

"I said, 'You must be so lonely.' And I said, 'It's pathetic watching you walking up the aisle at St. Paul's with Lord Mountbatten's coffin in front.' [The service was in Westminster Abbey.] I said, you know, 'It's ghastly. You need someone beside you.' Ugh! Wrong word. Whereupon he leapt upon me, and started kissing me and everything. And I thought waaaaah.

You know. This isn't what people do. And he was all over me for the rest of the evening – followed me around, everything, a puppy. And um, yeah, I was flattered but I was very puzzled."

At the time, Diana was still an innocent teenager and Charles was dating her older sister Sarah who was, to use Diana's favourite phrase, "all over him like a bad rash".

When she was seventeen, she wrote to her nanny Mary Clarke, saying: "For the last few years, Jane, Charles and I have been trying to marry off Sarah to various men but have failed in every direction. We even thought Prince Charles might have been in the running but were relieved when that passed."

When Charles's attention turned to her, Diana was surprised.

"Gee, he's thirty-two," said Diana. "I'm only nineteen. I never thought he'd ever look twice at me."

Elsewhere, when asked about the age difference, she said: "Never really thought about it."

Despite their fumbling first encounter, Diana fell hard for Charles, though he had a lot to learn in the boyfriend department.

"He wasn't consistent with his courting abilities," she complained. "He'd ring me up every day for a week, and then he wouldn't speak to me for three weeks. Very odd. And I accepted that. I thought fine. Well, he knows where I am if he wants me. And then the thrill when he used to ring up was so immense and intense. Drive the other three girls in my flat crazy. But it was odd."

However, she did feel the pity for him. After a date with Charles, she would tell her flatmates, "It's appalling the way they push him around," and "They work him too hard!"

Nevertheless, when Charles invited her to a shooting weekend to Sandringham, her flatmates teased her that she was going to be the next queen of England. Wringing out a floor cloth, she said: "I doubt it. Can you see me swanning around in kid gloves and a ball-gown?"

Pretty soon rumours about their courtship abounded. Unguarded, Diana told a reporter from the Press Association: "I'd like to marry soon. What woman doesn't want to marry eventually? Next year? Why not?"

But she retracted the statement the moment it appeared in the press.

"I never said anything about marriage," she insisted. "I am terribly worried about it. It's very upsetting."

It was her first encounter with the media.

From then on she became more circumspect. Speaking the *Sun*'s royal correspondent Harry Arnold: "You know I cannot say anything about the prince or my feelings for him. I am saying that off my own bat.

No one has told me to stay quiet."

Asked whether Charles had proposed, she said: "I can't say yes or no."

But the couple got caught out. In November 1980, the *Sunday Mirror* ran a story alleging that Diana had spent two nights with Charles aboard the royal train. Diana pleaded: "Please believe me. I've never been on that train. I have never even seen it."

She later denied telling a newspaper that she'd spent the nights of the alleged train incident because she had a hangover.

"I never get hangovers," she said.

After the announcement of the engagement, they were interviewed on television. Asked if they were in love, Diana answered "Of course", while Charles famously said: "Whatever in love means."

At the time she agreed, but this must have come as something of a disillusionment to a woman who averred: "The only reason for marriage is love."

Diana later remembered that Charles had used this caveat before. Seconds after she had accepted his proposal of marriage, she recalled: "I said: 'I love you so much, I love you so much.' He said: 'Whatever love means.'"

But the remark was overlooked in the rapture of the moment. She told friends: "He said: 'Will you marry me?' and I laughed. 'Yes, please.'"

Diana was clear in her own mind.

"It is what I wanted – it is what I want," she assured friends. "I know what I'm doing. I will be able to cope."

There was no doubt about their love in the eyes of onlookers. Diana is widely quoted on the internet saying: "I loved Charles. And he loved me – very, very much. To say that he didn't is wrong, totally wrong." It has not been possible to track down the source of this quote though. However, all the red tops carried her saying on the occasion of her engagement in February 1981: "With Charles beside me, I can't go wrong."

Writing to Mary Clarke from Buckingham Palace, two weeks before her wedding: "Not long to go now and about time too! Six months of being engaged is quite something and definitely to be avoided! All the family in complete overdrive and a lot of non speaks going on!!"

At a garden party honouring the Year of the Disabled Person, Diana asked a guest: "Will you be watching the wedding?"

"Yes," he replied a little bewildered. "Will you?"

"No," she said with a laugh. "I'm in it."

Perhaps she had a foreboding. At a Buckingham Palace garden party, she said of the wedding: "I'm going to videotape it so I'll be able to run back over the best bits and rub out the part where I say 'I will.'"

With the wedding just two weeks away and the plans for the spectacular event now in place, Diana told a reporter: "I think I am realising now what it all means and it's making me more and more scared."

Watching the pre-wedding coverage on TV, she grew quite nervous. "Do I really have to go out in front of all these people?" she asked her seamstress.

The relationship was in trouble from the off. "Bulimia started the week after we got engaged," she said. "Charles had his hand on my waist and said you're getting a bit chubby, and that triggered something off."

Soon the eating disorder became a vital outlet.

"The first time I made myself sick I was so thrilled. It relieved me of tension."

Bearing in mind what Charles had said to her, she wanted to lose weight before the wedding.

"I'm not waddling up the aisle like a duck," she said.

Diana wanted to pull out of the marriage, but her sister Sarah said: "Bad luck, Duch" – the family's pet name for her – "your face is on the tea towels and you're too late to chicken out."

Overcome by the pressures of the impending

wedding – already billed "the wedding of the century" – Diana when in tears as she told her sister Jane: "All I want to do is marry Charles. I can't face all this. Look at everyone I can't go through with it."

When her old piano teacher visited, Diana told her: "In twelve days time, I shall no longer be me."

Despite everything, Diana managed to keep her sense of humour.

"Do you want to feel my engagement ring?" she asked a blind well-wisher a few days before the wedding, "I'd better not lose it before Wednesday, or they won't know who I am."

The day after Charles' stag night, she asked another in the crowd to keep an eye out for her fiancé.

"If he comes past, ask him why he's looking so pale," she said.

The night before the wedding an interview was broadcast where Diana said she was "looking forward to being a good wife". Asked if Charles been a great help in the recent months, she said: "Marvellous, oh, a tower of strength." Then she turned to him and added: "I had to say that because you are sitting there."

She also revealed how little she had to do with the arrangements for the wedding, making only one minor request.

"I've asked for one hymn, 'I Vow to Thee, My Country', which has always been my favourite since school days," she said

The hymn was also played at her funeral.

As it was, nothing went smoothly. "We had a wedding rehearsal yesterday," she said. "Everybody was fighting. I got my heels stuck in some grating in the cathedral and everybody said, 'Hurry up, Diana,' and I said, 'I can't. I'm stuck.'"

Asked what plans she had for the night before the wedding, Diana told an interviewer she planned "to be tucked up in bed, I think, early night".

Charles interjected: "Not allowed to see me anyway the night before."

"We might quarrel," Diana added.

Recalling what actually happened the night before her wedding, Diana said: "I had a very bad fit of bulimia. I ate everything I could possibly find, which amused my sister [Jane] because she was staying with me at Clarence House and nobody understood what was going on there. It was all very hush hush. I was sick as a parrot that night. It was such an indication of what was going on."

Diana's stepmother Raine's mother was the grand-dame of romantic novelists Dame Barbara Cartland.

She was not invited to the royal wedding.

"Her false eyelashes look like two crows flying into the White Cliffs of Dover," Diana once reportedly remarked.

On her way to Clarence house, her Royal Protection Officer told her: "I just want you to know that this is the last night of freedom in your life so make the most of it."

These words filled her with foreboding. "They felt like a sword through my heart."

At her old flat at Coleherne Court, she left a note saying: "For God's sake ring me up – I'm going to need you."

It was impossible to sleep. "All night people were sitting out on the steps singing 'Rule Britannia', and every kind of thing. It really was remarkable, and I found myself standing in the window with tears pouring down my face.

The rejoicing surrounding the royal wedding did little to help. About one million people are reported to have flocked to London to see the ceremony, but Diana got cold feet. She said: "I cannot marry him. I cannot do this." She was eventually talked around by her family.

Arriving at the steps of the cathedral, she asked, "Is he here yet?"

Humour held it together.

"I thought the whole thing was hysterical, getting married," she said, but by the time she was walking down the aisle: "I was very, very deathly calm. I felt as though I was a lamb going to the slaughter."

On the way to the altar, she kept an eye out for her rival.

"As I walked up the aisle I was looking for Camilla," she said. "I knew she was there, of course. I looked for her."

However, she also said: "I remember being so in love with my husband that I couldn't take my eyes off him. I just absolutely thought I was the luckiest girl in the world. He was going to look after me. Well, I was wrong on that."

Diana would later recall her wedding day as "the most emotionally confusing day of my life".

There was no escaping the spectre of Camilla. As Diana would say later: "Walking down the aisle, I spotted Camilla pale grey, veiled pillbox hat… saw it all her son Tom standing on a chair. To this day, you know a vivid memory."

But, after spotting her, Diana recalled thinking: "There we are. That's it. Let's hope that's all over with."

It was not. During their honeymoon, she noted that Charles carried two photographs of Camilla in his diary, she said.

Meanwhile the ordeal of the ceremony had to be endured.

"It was heaven, amazing, wonderful," she said, "though I was so nervous when I was walking up the aisle that I swore my knees would knock and make a noise."

At the altar, Charles whispered to Diana, simply, "You look wonderful."

"Wonderful for you," she replied.

Then her nerves got the worst of her. During her vows, she muddled the order of Charles's names – Charles Philip Arthur George – saying: "I, Diana Frances, take thee, Philip Charles Arthur George."

On the steps of St Paul's Diana found herself facing unreasonable expectations.

"The public… they wanted a fairy princess to come and touch them, and everything will turn into gold and all their worries would be forgotten. Little did they realise that the individual was crucifying herself inside because she didn't think she was good enough."

Nevertheless, she enjoyed the wedding crowds: "It's wonderful to see people's enthusiastic reaction. A mass of smiling faces. It's most rewarding and gives me a tremendous boost."

Once the wedding was over, she was undaunted.

"After all this fuss, I am sure we will live happily ever after," she said.

It was, perhaps, wishful thinking.

Even so she was as yet undaunted. "I had tremendous hope in me, which was slashed by day two."

On the second night, Charles got out a novel by his mentor South African philosopher and adventurer Laurens van der Post. He bought seven of them on the honeymoon and they had to analyse them over lunch every day.

At Balmoral too: "He would read Laurens van der Post or Jung to me, and bear in mind I hadn't a clue about psychic powers or anything."

Charles was less than impressed with Diana's knowledge of literature. When he asked if she'd read Kipling's *Just So Stories*, she replied: "Just so what?"

On another occasion, she admitted: "I enjoy Danielle Steel's books, but my husband disapproves. He doesn't like me reading light novels."

In an effort to improve herself, she became an avid reader. "I've got a lot to learn. I've got 101 books sitting by my bedside – piles of books – absolutely gripped."

Later when Charles suggested that she should become better informed so that they could have more intelligent conversations, she retorted, "The whole world thinks I'm fine just as I am. That ought to be enough for you."

There was a high point on honeymoon cruise though, when she happened upon a group of men wearing only towels around their waists.

"It's all right. I'm a married woman now, aren't I?" she said.

But Diana continued to suffer from bulimia on her honeymoon.

"It was rife, four times a day on the *Britannia*," she said. "Anything I could find I would gobble up and be sick two minutes later very tired. So, of course, that slightly got the mood swings going in the sense that one minute one would be happy, next blubbing one's eyes out."

Then it was on to Balmoral.

"Everyone was there to welcome us," she said. "Then the realisation set in. My dreams were appalling. At night I dreamt of Camilla the whole time."

Nevertheless, at the honeymoon press conference, asked what she thought of married life, she replied: "Highly recommended."

Had she cooked breakfast?

"I don't eat breakfast," she said.

There was no one she could turn to for help, least of all her nearest and dearest.

"I hated myself so much, I didn't think I was good enough for Charles," she said. "My husband made me feel so inadequate in every possible way. Every time I came up for air, he pushed me back down again."

The result was self-harm. "I was trying to cut my wrists with razor blades," she admitted. "We were trying to hide that from everybody... I was just so desperate."

It had begun after their annual trip to Scotland, which she cut short to return to London.

"I had to come down for treatment because I was so depressed," she said.

By the time the marriage was five months old she was feeling "desperate" and although she was already pregnant with Prince William she felt inadequate.

"Charles said I was 'crying wolf' and I said I just felt so desperate and I was crying my eyes out. He said, 'I'm not going to listen... I'm going riding now'. So I threw myself down the stairs, bearing in mind I was carrying a child. The Queen came out and saw me and was horrified, shaking she's so frightened. I knew I wasn't going to lose the baby. Charles went out riding, and when he came back it was total dismissal."

Before they were married, she was asked what interests she shared with Charles.

"All outdoor pursuits except riding," she replied.

As a child she had fallen from her pony and broke her arm. After that, she never again wanted to find herself on horseback. She told one of her former flatmates: "I even prayed to God to give me the courage to ride again. I desperately wanted to please Charles, to be able to ride with him because I realised it was so important for him, for us. And yet I just couldn't relax. I don't know why. I just couldn't. Sometimes I would cry alone at night about it."

The Royal Family was a horsey lot, so she received a lot of encouragement.

"A vast amount of people are trying to get me onto a horse and it looks as though I might, since it's the one time I'd actually be able to be with the husband," she wrote to her former nanny, Mary Clarke. "I took him to Althorp for the w/e which was alright, except that in our short stay we managed to break two smart chairs and a glass window. Raine didn't know how to take that!"

Later Diana threw herself in to a glass cabinet in Kensington Palace.

"Once I picked up his penknife off his dressing table and scratched myself down my chest and both thighs. There was a lot of blood." She said Charles had "no reaction whatsoever".

She managed to keep her distress to herself, confiding to her Mary Clarke: "I adore being married and having someone to devote my time, however, I do get annoyed at not being able to do my washing and general ironing! I know sister Sarah would adore that situation! I might even have to learn to ride a horse as it is the only time I will ever see my husband on his own…."

Diana felt inadequate was partially because she still saw herself as a bit part – rather than the superstar she became.

"I see my role as supporting my husband whenever I can and always being behind him, encouraging him," she said in her first television interview in 1985. "It's most important being a mother and a wife – that's what I try to achieve. Whether I do is another thing, but I do try."

Despite it all, she called the early 1980s "my early fairy period". She was still desperate and would do anything to make the marriage work.

When oil billionaire Armand Hammer told her: "You know, I can't say no to the Prince, whatever he asks me to do. I have so much confidence in him that if he asked me to jump through that window there, I think I'd jump through", she smiled and replied: "Well, I'd jump right after you!"

The marriage was also beginning to cool when Diana danced onstage at the Royal Opera House with Wayne Sleep, while Charles looked on. She turned him and said laughingly, "Beats the wedding."

After eight curtain calls, Sleep said: "It's best to leave them wanting more. Now bow to the royal box."

"I'm not bowing to him, he's my hubby," she said.

She wrote to thank him. The letter said: "Now I understand the buzz you get from performing. It's fantastic."

Later, the press hounded him, thinking – wrongly – that he had AIDS. Diana thought they went after him because of their friendship.

"It must be awful knowing me," she said.

In 1991, Diana recorded a series out tapes about her failing marriage and her relations with the Royal Family.

"I want people to understand the torment and anguish going on inside my head. It was a desperate cry for help," she said. "I'm not spoilt. I just need to be allowed to adapt to my new position."

These tapes were eventually aired in America by NBC in 2004.

She also accused the Queen of spreading stories about their marital problems, always taking Charles's side.

"He definitely told her about my bulimia", she claimed. "She told everybody that was the reason our marriage cracked up."

Nevertheless Diana turned to her mother-in-law for help. According to Diana, the Queen said: "I don't know what you should do. Charles is hopeless."

Love

Diana was frank about her disappointment with the sexual side of her marriage. The very idea that she might have had a fulfilling relationship foundered on the second day of the honeymoon, when Charles spent the day reading. In 1992, she said: "It fizzled out about seven years ago."

That was shortly after the birth of Prince Harry. Although she was not vastly experienced in this area, she found it strange.

"Instinct told me, it was just so odd," she said.

But then, it was never a relationship of high passion.

"There was never a requirement for it from his case," she said. "Sort of a once every three weeks look about it and I kept thinking... and then I followed a pattern. He used to see his lady once every three weeks before we got married."

It was then that she realised that Charles was continuing his relationship with his former girl-friend Camilla Parker-Bowles. Diana took the matter up with him: "I remember saying to my husband, you know, 'Why, why is this lady around?' And he said, 'Do you seriously expect me to be the only

Prince of Wales who never had a mistress.'"

Even though Camilla was married to Andrew Parker Bowles, her relationship with Charles was a constant torment to Diana.

"Charles placed many of his calls to Camilla from his bathtub," she said. "Once, after breast-feeding William, I heard him on the phone saying whatever happens, I will always love you. I told him later that I had listened at the bathroom door and we had a filthy row."

An interesting account of another incident appears on the Princess Diana Remembered website:

"On finding the four-poster bed she and Charles had shared was unmade, the sheets crumpled and slept in, the Princess then ran into the spare bedrooms; none was disturbed.

"'I was hysterical. It was clear the main bed, our bed, my marital bed, had been slept in by two people. I went downstairs and screamed at him for sleeping with that woman in my bed. He wouldn't answer. I was shouting at him and crying but he wouldn't say anything. I kept asking him why he was bonking her. It was the worst moment ever. I felt like it was all over. I knew for sure he was sleeping with that bitch. I seriously thought about topping myself there and then. I knew there was no chance. I knew he loved her and not me – and always had done.'"

Soon she realised that she had lost him forever. When she became pregnant for a second time, she said: "By then I knew he had gone back to his lady, but somehow we managed to have Harry."

In 1989, she had confronted Camilla at her sister's birthday party, interrupting a conversation between Charles, Camilla and another male guest.

"I said to the two men, 'OK, boys, I'm just going to have a quick word with Camilla and I'll be up in a minute'," she said. "And they shot upstairs like chickens with no heads and I could feel, upstairs, all hell breaking loose – 'What is she going to do?'"

Diana then told Camilla: "I would just like you to know that I know exactly what is going on between you and Charles. I wasn't born yesterday."

According to Diana, Camilla's response was "very interesting".

"She said to me: 'You've got everything you ever wanted. You've got all the men in the world fall in love with you and you've got two beautiful children, what more do you want?'

"So I said, 'I want my husband'. And I said, 'I'm sorry I'm in the way ... and it must be hell for both of you. But I do know what's going on. Don't treat me like an idiot. Leave my husband alone.'"

Burning with jealousy, Diana turned to her bodyguard Ken Wharfe to keep tabs on her husband's movements.

"You know about Camilla, don't you?" she told him.

"I don't know how to deal with it. It's there and I can't do anything about it."

Eventually, Diana consulted a doctor about her feelings that had now turned suicidal.

"He said to me, 'How many times have you tried to get rid of yourself?' and I thought, 'Wow!' So I said about five or six times," she recounted. "He said, 'How?' and I said all the various instruments I tried – threats, all the rest of it, glass, the lot. And he said, 'I can get you better in no time at all – the problem lies with your husband'. And he said, 'In six months time, you'll be a completely different person.'"

At the end of her marriage, Diana found herself isolated, alone and rued: "There's just nobody to physically scream at. Or someone to put their arms around me and just listen."

It took its toll.

"There's no better way to dismantle a personality than to isolate it," she said.

Nevertheless, she was determined to embrace the destiny that she felt certain awaited her.

"I knew that something profound was coming my way and I was just treading water, waiting for it," she said. "I didn't know what it was. I didn't know where it was. I didn't know if it was coming next year or next month. But I knew I was different from my friends in where I was going."

Diana found a new strength inside herself after co-oper-ating with biographer Andrew Morton, author of *Diana: Her True Story in He Own Words*. Asked why she had done that, she replied: "I was at the end of my tether. I was desperate. I think I was so fed up with being seen as someone who was a basket-case, because I am a very strong person and I know that causes complications in the system that I live in."

Asked about the Royal Family's reaction to the book, Diana said: "I think they were shocked and horri-fied and very disappointed."

It put her at odds with the Palace.

"I think every strong woman in history has had to walk down a similar, and I think it's the strength that causes the confusion and the fear. Why is she strong? Where does she get it from? Where is she taking it? Where is she going to use it?"

They were afraid of her.

"Here was a strong woman doing her bit," she said, "and where was she getting her strength from to con-tinue?

Her fate, she soon realised involved her capacity to love. Frequently listed among her most inspiring quotes is: "I think the biggest disease the world suffers from in this day and age is the disease of people feeling unloved. I know that I can give love for a minute, for half an hour, for a day, for a month, but I can give. I am very happy to do that, I want to do that."

Elsewhere, this is rendered: "The worse illness of

our time is that so many people have to suffer from never having been loved."

Clearly, it is informed by deep personal experience – both of loving and being unloved. According to her confidante Lady Bowker: "She said that she was always unwanted: unwanted as a baby because her parents had wanted a boy, and unwanted in her marriage because Charles loved someone else. She was pining for love and affection because she was starved of them for so long."

Diana told her voice coach Peter Settelen: "My parents, they never said they loved me."

She never felt loved and there was no physical affection beyond a peck on the cheek.

"There was always a kiss there, no hugs or anything like that," she said.

Despite attracting the adoration of the world, Diana often found herself lonely and unloved.

"Loneliness is the worst pain in this world," she said. "It constantly eats away the person's heart, and can cause the person to hate, to feel enraged. It is like a wound of the heart; the type of wounds that cannot go away with a kiss or a hug. The only thing that can make this great pain go away is love and compassion, another human heart to pull them out of this hell."

Elsewhere she said: "There seems to be a growing feeling of discontent, of emptiness in many peoples' lives. While an overwhelming sense of loss and isolation undermines their efforts to survive and cope with the complexities of modern life. They know something crucial is lacking."

What made this so poignant is that it was a sense of emptiness, loss and isolation that she, at times, had plainly shared.

It was a theme she would return to in her public pronouncements: "The misery of living without love, the pain of being unloved. There's no substitute for affection and I urge everyone to help that message grow. And together we may stem the flood of vulnerable souls by helping them to find their stable platforms."

Admitting adultery with dashing cavalry officer James Hewitt, she said: "Yes, I adored him. Yes, I was in love with him. But I was very let down."

This was because he had co-operated with author Anna Pasternak on the book *Princess in Love*.

"It was very distressing for me that a friend of mine, who I had trusted, made money out of me."

She really minded about that.

"And he'd rung me up ten days before it arrived in the bookshops to tell me that there was nothing to worry about," she said, "and I believed him, stupidly."

Unlike Camilla, Diana said: "I decline to go fox hunting."

Diana had little time for hunting of any kind and did not want her children to be photographed with a gun in their hand.

"I told William, 'Remember, there is always

someone in a high-rise flat who doesn't want you to shoot Bambis'," she said.

However, royal protocol demanded that both her sons serve in the army.

There were rumours that the sport she preferred was rugby, after taking on England captain Will Carling on as her personal trainer. Although he was smuggled in and out of the palace under a blanket in the back of the car, both insisted they did not have an affair.

Diana also refused to accept any of the blame when Carling's marriage to TV presenter Julia Carling broke up.

"I won't apologise," she said. "I have no reason to."

Diana knew she had to tread carefully.

"If I date single men," she said, "the relationship ends as soon as the press find out. They move in, digging under every stone to find out everything they can about the poor person. If I date married men – even purely socially – I'm labelled a marriage breaker."

In 1985, Diana fell in love with Sergeant Barry Mannakee of the Royal Protection Squad, a handsome married father of two.

"I was quite happy to give it all up... just to go off and live with him. Can you believe it? And he kept saying he thought it was a good idea, too."

She told Peter Settelen: "I tell you one of the biggest crutches of my life, which I don't find easy to discuss, was when I was 24, 25. I fell deeply in love with somebody who worked in this environment. And he was the greatest fellow I have ever had. I was always waiting around trying to see him. I just, you know, wore my heart on my sleeve. I was only happy when he was around."

He provided the intimacy she was not getting from Charles. But the relationship ended in disaster.

"It got so difficult and eventually he had to go," she said. "It was all found out and he was chucked out."

Two years later, Mannakee died in a motorbike accident. Diana thought Charles was deliberately cruel in telling her in the limousine on the way to the Cannes Film Festival.

"Charles told me that he was killed in a motorbike accident. And that was the biggest blow of my life, I must say. That was a real killer. And he just jumped it on me like that and I wasn't able to do anything," she said. "I just sat there all day going through this huge high-profile visit to Cannes. Thousands of press. Just devastated, just devastated."

Diana believed he had been killed to prevent a scandal.

"I think he was bumped off. But I will never know."

Afterwards she was haunted by nightmares.

"I used to have really disturbing dreams about him. He was unhappy, wherever he's gone to."

She managed to track down the cemetery where he had been buried.

"I went to put some flowers on his grave," she said,

only to discover he had been cremated and his ashes scattered. "He was just chucked over the ground. That absolutely appalled me. But there we are, I wasn't in a position to do anything about it."

Nevertheless she left the flowers.

"The day I did that, the dreams stopped. It's strange, isn't it, like a sort of recognition," she said. "I should never have played with fire and I did. And I got very burned."

After her divorce, she was asked whether she would ever marry again.

"Who would take me on?" she asked forlornly. "I have so much baggage. Anyone who takes me out to dinner has to accept the fact that their business will be raked over in the papers. Photographers will go through their dustbins. I think I am safer alone."

At the time, she had just broken up with Pakistani-born heart surgeon Hasnat Khan – aka "my dishy doctor" – after a two-year relationship conducted largely in secret.

"Diana was madly in love with Hasnat Khan and wanted to marry him," Jemima Khan told *Vanity Fair*. "Even if that meant living in Pakistan, and that's one of the reasons why we became friends."

Diana visited Jemima twice in Pakistan to help fund-raise for the hospital where her former husband Imran Khan – a distant cousin of Diana's lover – worked.

"Both times she also went to meet his family secret-ly to discuss the possibility of marriage to Hasnat," she said. "She wanted to know how hard it had been for me to adapt to life in Pakistan."

After Diana died, Khan was asked by the police about the possibility of them marrying. He said that he had told Diana: "It was a ridiculous idea."

Soon after she began her relationship with millionaire department store heir Dodi Fayed. Khan kept quiet about his relationship with Diana, until he heard about Dodi.

"When I found out I was really mad, mad as hell," he said.

After falling in love with Dodi, the *Washington Post* reported that she was "telling friends" ("generally the code here for Princess Diana telling a reporter"): "It's time I started getting a life. He is the man who will take me out of one world and into another. I trust him. I think he can provide everything I need."

The *Daily Mirror* quoted her saying: "I just love his gentleness, his kindness, and his almost dull way of living. For someone like me, who has lived a goldfish-bowl type of existence, I can't tell you how comforting that is. I like the way he sends flowers. I like the way he conducts himself, not only with me but with women in general. The days of hiding are over."

The *Post* pointed out that the "women in general included Brooke Shields, Britt Ekland, actress Valerie Perrine, Tina Sinatra and American model Suzanne Gregard, who Fayed was married to for eight months in 1986. And his "dull way of living" involved two Ferraris, at least one vintage Rolls-Royce, a $23 million yacht, a Sikorsky helicopter, a Gulfstream jet, a castle in the Scottish Highlands and other homes in Switzerland, New York, Dubai, Geneva, Genoa and London. The previous Thursday he had dinner brought in on silver platters for the two of them at his apartment across from Hyde Park. His family owned the building, along with a slew of other buildings in Mayfair, one of the world's most expensive neighbourhoods.

"Why are the media so anti-Dodi?" asked Diana, naïvely. "Is it because he's a millionaire?"

Diana was very protective of her new lover.

"I'm very upset at the criticism of him," she told friends in St Tropez. "I've known him for years and we have been close friends for the last five. It was all cleared with Buckingham Palace long ago."

However, Prince Philip made no secret of his feelings about his former daughter-in-law's liaison with Fayed Jnr, calling him as an "oily bed-hopper".

But Diana's passion was undimmed. On the phone to model Cindy Crawford the day before she died, Diana said: "For the first time in my life, I can say that I am truly happy. Dodi is a fantastic man. He fills me with attention and care. I feel once more loved.

After Diana died, friends told the newspapers that she was blissfully happy in her last days with Dodi Fayed. The conversations between the two lovers were full of laughter. However, she grew angry when he listed the expensive gifts he had bought her.

"I don't want expensive gifts," she said. "It makes me uneasy. I don't want to be bought. I have everything I want. I just want someone to be there for me, to make me feel safe and secure."

"Her dark side was that of a wounded, trapped animal and her bright side was that of a luminous being," said friend Rosa Monckton. "If she had found – as she appeared to have with Dodi – some emotional stability, then the luminous side might have prevailed."

However, expensive gifts had been involved. On the day she died, Fayed had given Diana a ring worth £130,000, while Diana had given Dodi a gold cigar clipper inscribed "With love from Diana" and cuff links left to her by her father, the late Earl Spencer.

In an accompanying letter, written in thick fountain pen on Kensington Palace notepaper and dated 13 August 1997, Diana wrote: "Darling Dodi, these cuf- flinks were the very last gift from the man I loved most in the world, my father. They are given to you as I know how much joy it would give him to know they were in such safe and special hands. Fondest love, Diana."

Such baubles meant little to her. Princess Diana famous- ly said: "They say it is better to be poor and happy than rich and miserable, but how about a compromise like moderately rich and just moody?"

Flying out to Bosnia, Dodi insisted that she take the

Fayeds' private jet. Accompanying her was *Daily Telegraph* journalist Bill Deedes, who made a comment about her having influential friends. She looked him in the eye and said: "My investment portfolio from the divorce settlement is doing very well, thank you, Lord Deedes."

Commenting on the pink seats and the green pile carpet with pharaohs' heads on it, she commented: "Isn't it awful?"

When the air hostess brought her a tin of Beluga caviar, a present from Dodi, she gave it to her friend Rosa Monckton, saying: "You take this, Rosa. Give it to Dominic [Rosa's husband]." Adding with a giggle: "You see, I know I'll be having some at dinner tonight."

By the end Diana had reconciled her differences with Camilla Parker Bowles, who she had once dubbed "the rottweiller" and Tiggy Legge-Bourke, personal assistant to the prince who had looked after William and Harry in Diana's absence. "When you are happy you can forgive a great deal," said Lady Bowker, one of the princess more intimate confidantes.

"Elsa, I adore him. I have never been so happy," Diana told Bowker days before she died. "I feel protected and I have real love."

Though Diana had earlier thought that she would win Charles back from Camilla because she was "younger and more beautiful", her ex-husband's relationship with her rival had become a joke. When asked whether the initials "CC" on a gilt belt, meant Coco Chanel, Diana replied: "No… Camilla and Charles."

In the end, she realised that Camilla had been the love of Charles's life and she had been a discreet and loyal friend.

"I always thought Camilla was the perfect love match with Charles," she said.

As for Tiggy – who had once raised Diana's ire for referring to William and Harry as "my babies" – she said: "She is devoted to the children and they are devoted to her. Because she gives them happiness, I now accept her."

Nevertheless, Diana was insistent: "A mother's arms are more comforting than anyone else's" – perhaps recalling her own childhood.

By then Diana had even reconciled herself with Charles. According to Bowker the princess was "closer to Prince Charles at the end than ever. She had real feeling for him. She was not 'in love' with him, but cared for him."

Diana had long been reconciled with Prince Philip. In 1992, he wrote in letter to her, saying: "If invited, I will always do my utmost to help you and Charles to the best of my ability, but I am quite ready to concede that I have no talents as a marriage counsellor!!!"

Diana replied: "Dearest Pa, I was particularly touched by your most recent letter which proved to me, if I didn't already know it, that you really do care. You are very modest about your marriage guidance skills and

I disagree with you. This last letter of yours showed great understanding and tact and I hope to be able to draw on your advice in the months ahead whatever they may bring."

On another occasion she wrote to him: "I was so immensely relieved to receive such a thoughtful letter as the one you sent to me showing such obvious willingness to help. With my fondest love, Diana."

In the end the gloves came off. According to Tina Brown, during the negotiations for the divorce, the Duke of Edinburgh warned: "If you don't behave, my girl, we'll take your title away."

She is said to have replied: "My title is a lot older than yours, Philip."

After "the most magical six days on the ocean waves" on board Dodi's father's yacht, her thank-you note to "Darling Dodi" read: "This comes with all the love in the world and as always a million heartfelt thanks for bringing such joy into this particular chick's life, from Diana x."

"Life is just a journey," said Diana, but not always one, like hers, that ended in tragedy. However, it was not a journey taken alone. When withdrawing from public life in 1993, she said: "I couldn't stand here today and make this sort of statement without acknowledging the heartfelt support I've been given by the public in general."

Being Royal

As a free spirit, Diana found herself stifled by the protocol at surrounded the Royal Family.

"From the first day I joined that family, nothing could be done naturally any more," she complained.

Princess Diana famously said: "I wear my heart on my sleeve." This was palpably true both in her private and public life, and it seems to be a trait common to newcomers to the Royal Family. During a multi-million dollar tour of America for Weightwatchers after her much-publicised divorce, Fergie, Duchess of York, said: "I'm a closet American – I wear my heart on my sleeve. I'm very open, where in Britain, it's stiff upper lip and don't speak about it.

"Only do what your heart tells you," was another of Princess Diana's much quoted maxims, though she admitted that it got her into trouble. Nevertheless, the heart was all important to her. She said: "I always knew I'd never be the next Queen. I'd like to be a queen of people's hearts, in people's hearts, but I don't see myself being Queen of this country. I don't think many people will want me to be Queen. Actually, when I say many people, I mean the establishment that I married into."

Clearly Princess Diana succeeded in becoming the queen of people's hearts and it gave her succour. Announcing her withdrawal from public life in December 1993, following her separation from Prince Charles, she told the audience: "Your kindness and affection have carried me through some of the most difficult periods, and always your love and affection have eased the journey. And for that I thanks you, from the bottom of my heart."

But then: "Being a princess isn't all it's cracked up to be."

Diana was humble in the face of the public affection heaped on her.

"So many people supported me through my public life and I will never forget them," she said. "I want to reassure all those people who have loved me and supported me throughout the last fifteen years that I'd never let them down. That is a priority to me…"

The reason was simple. She wanted to reassure the people, "the people that matter to me – the man on the street, because that's what matters more than anything else."

It was always the ordinary people who concerned Diana. "The people that I care about are the people out there on the street," she said. "I can identify with them."

"The greatest problem in the world today is intolerance," said Princess Diana. "Everyone is so intolerant of each other."

This was widely interpreted as Diana expressing her support for gay rights, after she had visited a gay bar with Freddie Mercury. However, Diana suffered more than her fair share of intolerance herself. Prince Philip intolerance of her was widely reported. When the story of her affair with James Hewitt came out, he would say to anyone who would care to listen: "Well, what do you expect?"

Jonathan Dimbleby's *The Prince of Wales: A Biography* also pointed out Charles "tendency to grumble", his short temper, his self-centredness, his intolerance, his vanity and his jealousy of his wife's popularity.

"With the media attention came a lot of jealousy," she said. "A great deal of complicated situations arose because of that.

On the occasion of Charles's 50th birthday party at Highgrove, Diana said: "Wouldn't it be funny if I suddenly came out of the birthday cake?"

Becoming royal meant that Diana had to steer clear of politics. In 1995, she said: "I'm not a political animal, but I think the biggest disease this world suffers from in this day and age is the disease of people feeling unloved."

A year later, visiting a ward for landmine victims in

a hospital in Angola, she said: "I am not a political figure. The fact is I am a humanitarian figure and always will be." And she dismissed the sniping from MPs, saying: "I saw the row at Westminster as merely a distraction which meant things went off the rails for five minutes and went back on again. It's not helpful things like that but it does happen when a campaign is entwined in a political issue. I understand that."

A month after that, she said: "I am not a political figure, not do I want to be one; but I give with my heart."

During an emotional speech at the National Geographic Society in London in June 1997, she said: "I am not a political figure. My interests are humanitarian."

She repeated the sentiment in the *Daily Mirror* on 6 August, defending her visit to Angola: "Some people chose to interpret my visit as a political statement. But it was not."

There was also petty disharmony in the royal marriage.

"Fashion is not my thing at all," she said, "but if Prince Charles chose an outfit, I'd say: 'Go with the other one!'"

This is an astonishing statement for a woman whose style and dress-sense was picked over and emulated by millions all around the world. For her years in public life, she was seen as a leader of fashion.

Charles gave as good as he got. Getting ready for a

public engagement, he would say "Not that dress again", undermining her confidence. Describing their relationship, Diana said: "It's just so difficult. So complicated. He makes my life real, real torture."

Nevertheless: "We struggled along. We did our engagements together. And in our private life it was obviously turbulent."

Martin Bashir said that Jonathan Dimbleby's biography of the Prince of Wales made him out to be a great thinking, a man with a tremendous range of interests.

"What did he think of your interests?" asked Bashir.

"Well, I don't think I was allowed to have any. I think that I've always been the 18-year-old girl he got engaged to, so I don't think I've been given any credit for growth. And, my goodness, I've had to grow."

She complained that she was always the target of criticism.

"Anything good I ever did nobody ever said a thing, never said, 'well done', or 'was it OK?'" she said. "But if I tripped up, which invariably I did, because I was new at the game, a ton of bricks came down on me."

It was a perennial problem. "I was thrown into the deep end.... Nobody ever helped me at all. They'd be there to criticise me, but never there to say 'Well done.'"

The split from Charles caused difficulties for the Royal

Family.

"I was the separated wife of the Prince of Wales, I was a problem, fullstop," she said. "Never happened before, what do we do with her?"

This was not entirely true. It had happened before. While Prince of Wales, the future George IV married Caroline of Brunswick-Lüneburg, though he was already secretly married to the widow Maria Fitzherbert. George and Caroline separated nine months later, after the birth of their only child, Princess Charlotte. Rumours circulated about her sex life. A committee of the Privy Council was set up to conduct the so-called "Delicate Investigation". In 1805, it acquitted her of charges of having a son by another man.

After George ascended to throne, he tried to dissolve the marriage to prevent her becoming queen. A bill was put before parliament and witnesses were called who gave salacious details of her love life. These were lapped up by the public and Caroline became so popular that, although the bill was passed by the House of Lords, it was not put before the Commons as there was little prospect that they would pass it. Caroline joked that she had indeed committed adultery once – with the husband of Mrs Fitzherbert.

At the coronation, the doors of Westminster Abbey were slammed in her face. She died nineteen days later. Huge crowds turned out when her body was transported back to Brunswick, forcing the cortège to travel through Westminster and the City.

Diana might well have taken a leaf out of Caroline's book. Asked whether she could be packed off somewhere quietly, ever mindful of her duty, Diana said of herself: "She won't go quietly, that's the problem. I'll fight to the end, because I believe that I have a role to fulfil, and I've got two children to bring up."

In December 1992, in the face of concerted pressure by the Royal Family, Diana agreed to a legal separation.

"We had struggled to keep it going, but obviously we'd both run out of steam," she said. "My husband asked for the separation and I supported it."

Her feelings on the occasion?

"Deep, deep, profound sadness."

Diana said that 28 February 1996 – the day she agreed to an uncontested divorce – was "the saddest day of my life". There followed haggling over what titles she could keep.

"I did not want this divorce, but I have agreed to it," she said. "Now they are playing ping-pong with me."

They had already played other games with her.

"It was, you know, if we are going to divorce, my husband would hold more cards than I would, it was very much a poker game, chess game."

In the end, she was stripped of the honorific "Her Royal Highness". According to the *New York Times* the queen had wanted her to keep it, but Charles insisted that she be stripped of it. It would mean that she was officially obliged to curtsey to him – and even to her own children.

"Don't worry, Mummy," William was reported saying. "I will give it back to you one day when I am king."

Only five years earlier, she had told *Good Housekeeping* magazine: "I am never going to get divorced and that's that. Whatever people may think and say, I am very happy, thank you very much."

The failure of the royal marriage had damaged Charles's regal prospects too.

"I know Charles will never be King and I will never be Queen," Diana said. "William will take our place. I would hope that my husband would go off, go away with his lady and sort that out. Then leave me and the children to carry the Wales name through to the time that William ascends the throne."

Diana was not alone in expecting the crown to skip a generation.

"All my hopes are on William now. I try to din it into him about the media – the dangers and how he must understand and handle it. It's too late for the rest of the family. But William, I think, has it."

She would be there to guide him on his way.

"I will help him to adapt to a changing world, to learn how to deal with and communicate with people. I am not against the Monarchy, why would I wish to destroy my children's future?"

After all, she was all too well aware of the pitfalls.

"For me, it was terrifying. I hadn't got a clue what I was meant to be doing. I don't want William and Harry suffering in the way I did," she said.

Following her separation, Diana was forced to cut back on her charity work. Announcing this, she still found time to thank her mother- and father-in-law.

"At the end of this year, when I have completed my diary of official engagements, I will be reducing the extent of the public life I have led so far," she said. "I attach great importance to my charity work and intend to focus on a smaller range of areas in the future. Over the next few months I will be seeking a more suitable way of combining a meaningful public role with, hopefully, a more private life. My first priority will continue to be our children, William and Harry, who deserve as much love, care and attention as I am able to give, as well as an appreciation of the tradition into which they were born. I would also like to add that this decision has been reached with the full understanding of the Queen and the Duke of Edinburgh, who have always shown me kindness and support."

There was no mention of Charles. Privately, she told a friend: "My husband's side have made my life hell for the last year."

Even in her devastating interview on *Panorama* she put in a good word for her husband and the monarchy. Diana concluded by saying: "I don't sit here with resentment: I sit here with sadness because a marriage hasn't worked. I sit here with hope because there's a future ahead, a future for my husband, a future for myself and a future for the monarchy."

A month later came the official announcement that the Queen had written to them, advising them to divorce.

Looking back as a mother of two and a player on the world stage, Diana realised how ill-prepared she was for the pressures incumbent on her as a member of the Royal Family.

"At the age of nineteen, you always think you're prepared for everything, and you think you have the knowledge of what's coming ahead," she said. "But although I was daunted at the prospect at the time, I felt I had the support of my husband-to-be."

"I wasn't daunted, and am not daunted by the responsibilities that that role creates. It was a challenge, it is a challenge."

As for becoming Queen: "It was never at the forefront of my mind when I married my husband: it was a long way off that thought."

Indeed she had had no real desire to become a princess. She was all too familiar with royal ways, having grown up on the Sandringham estate in a house rented from the Queen.

"I've known her since I was tiny, so meeting it was no big deal," she said. "I kept thinking, 'Look at the life they have, how awful.'"

Not only had Diana known the Queen since she was small, Scottish clergyman the Reverend Douglas Lister, former military chaplain to Earl Spencer, claimed that Di's father had once wooed Elizabeth when she was heir to the throne, but the Royal Family reportedly quashed the affair as he was considered unsuitable.

"He came to see me because he needed someone to talk to," said Lister. "He was in love with her and I think she had similar feelings for him."

For Charles's 30th birthday party, Diana was invited to Buckingham Palace.

"I wasn't at all intimidated by the surroundings," she said. "I thought, amazing place."

However, she was intimidated on her first trip to Balmoral.

"I was terrified – shitting bricks," she said.

Mr and Mrs Parker-Bowles were there.

Later she was invited to Windsor.

"I arrived about five o'clock and he sat me down and said: 'I've missed you so much.' But there was never anything tactile about him. It was extraordinary, but I didn't have anything to go by because I had never had a boyfriend. I'd always kept them away, thought they were all trouble – and I couldn't handle it emotionally, I was very screwed up, I thought."

It was then that he asked her to marry him.

"I remember thinking, 'This is a joke,' and I said:

'Yeah, OK,' and laughed. He was deadly serious. He said: 'You do realize that one day you will be Queen.' And a voice said to me inside: 'You won't be Queen but you'll have a tough role.' So I thought 'OK,' so I said: 'Yes.' I said: 'I love you so much, I love you so much.' He said: 'Whatever love means.'"

But there was a mismatch from the start.

"In my immaturity, which was enormous, I thought that he was very much in love with me, which he was, but he always had a sort of besotted look about him, looking back at it, but it wasn't the genuine sort. 'Who was this girl who was so different?' but he couldn't understand it because his immaturity was quite big in that department too. For me it was like a call of duty, really – to go and work with the people."

The shock of becoming a member of the Royal Family was enormous. "I didn't have any idea what I let myself in for," she said. "One day I was going to work on a Number 9 bus and the next I was a princess."

She got no help from courtiers at the palace.

"No one sat me down with a piece of paper and said: 'This is what is expected of you.'"

Diana was very conscious of what the public wanted of her though. "Here was a fairytale story that everybody wanted to work."

But she was cut off from anyone who could help her.

"It was isolating," she said, "but it was also a situation where you couldn't indulge in feeling sorry for yourself: you had to either sink or swim. And you had to learn that very fast... I swam."

Diana quickly got into the business of being a Royal. "Everywhere I go I smell fresh paint," she said.

However, during a trip to Australia in 1983, she told an admiring housewife: "I would trade places with you anytime."

It soon became very clear what the Royal Family expected of her too. To preserve the monarchy, she had to produce an heir. When she did so: "Everybody was thrilled to bits. It had been quite a difficult pregnancy. I hadn't been very well throughout it, so by the time William arrived, it was a great relief."

The pregnancy had been doubly difficult because Diana wanted the birth to be induced, but said it was difficult to schedule a birth date around Charles's polo matches.

As her time grew close, things got worse.

"It was a very, very difficult pregnancy indeed. I was sick the whole time," she said. "Almost every time I stood up I was sick. It was a very bad labour but when he arrived there was such great excitement. Everyone was as high as a kite."

But Diana's contribution was forgotten.

"There were endless pictures of the Queen, Queen Mother, Charles and William. I was excluded totally that day. I wasn't very well and I just blubbed my eyes out. William started crying too. Well, he just sensed that I wasn't exactly hunky-dory."

Her alienation from the Royal Family began when she suffered post-natal depression after the birth of Prince William.

"Maybe I was the first person ever to be in this family who ever had a depression, or was ever openly tearful," she said.

Just twenty years old, Diana's young life had taken another turn.

"In the space of a year my whole life had changed, turned upside down," she said. "It had its wonderful moments, but it also had challenging moments. And I could see where the rough edges needed to be smoothed."

Diana was perceived as a threat. "Once or twice, I've heard people say: 'Diana's out to destroy the monarchy,' which has bewildered me, because why would I want to destroy something that is my children's future?"

In fact, Diana saw herself as the saviour of the monarchy.

"It's vital the monarchy keeps in touch with the people," she said. "It's what I try and do...."

Indeed, she was adept at employing the common touch. According to Royal Protection Officer Ken Wharfe, she said: "Call me Diana, not Princess Diana."

She also thanked him for "taking her on".

"I'm sure I am seen as a poisoned chalice by you boys," she said.

The common touch was always on show. Visiting 150 people who had been evacuated from the homes during flooding in North Wales in 1990, she told one five-year-old girl: "Follow me around. You can be my lady-in-waiting."

In 1984, she visited a cancer patient in a Sue Ryder Home who complained he could not get his favourite beer.

"I'll bring you a bottle when I'm passing this way," said Diana. Better than her word, she sent him a case of twenty-four bottles.

When Charles broke his arm playing polo in 1990, Diana met car-crash victim Dean Woodward and stroked his forehead as he came out of a coma. The following year she dropped around to his council house to check up on his recovery, telling him on the doorstep: "I just thought I'd pop in for a cuppa."

She became a firm friend of the family and wrote to his mother Ivy when she heard she was ill, saying: "I am thinking of you constantly and you're in my prayers throughout the day. Keep strong."

To survive, Diana saw clearly that the monarchy had to change.

"I understand that change is frightening for people, especially if there is nothing to go to," she said. "It's best to stay where you are. I understand that."

To effect this change, she took William and Harry around homeless projects and to hospices – the "sorts of areas where I'm not sure anyone of that age in this family has been before".

There had to be a new relationship between the monarchy and the public.

"I think they could walk hand in hand, as opposed to be so distant," she said.

Diana was determined change the monarchy for the sake of William.

"I am altering it for him but in a subtle way," she said. "People aren't aware of it, but I am. I would never rattle the monarchy's cage, because when I think the mother-in-law has been doing it for forty years, who am I to come along and change it just like that?"

Already by 1985, Diana had had enough. "So I went to the top lady," she said. "And I was sobbing and I said, 'What do I do? I'm coming to you. What do I do?'"

The "top lady" was, of course, the Queen. Diana painted a piteous portrait of the emotion scene with the Queen in Buckingham Palace: "She said, 'I don't know what you should do. Charles is hopeless.' And that was it. That was help! So I didn't go back to her again for help because I don't go back again if I don't get it the first time, right. And so over the years, 'Diana never talks.' I never know what's going on. 'Silly girl.'"

Nevertheless, Diana had adapted to her royal role with good humour. Chatting to a friend on the phone, she said: "Sorry about the noise, I was trying to get my tiara on."

However, she found herself in competition with the stern figure of the Queen. Refusing a friend's offer of a fan when attending a royal garden party on a blazing July afternoon, she said: "I can't do that. My mother-in-law is going to be standing there with her handbag, gloves, stockings and shoes."

Diana once explained to Peter Stothard, editor of *The Times*, that the Royal Family were afraid of the rapport she had with the general public.

"My husband's father once sent me a long formal letter setting out the duties of the Princess of Wales," she said. "There was 'much more to it than being popular', he said. I sent him back a long letter in reply. He sent me a shorter one – and so on until I finally signed off with 'it's been so nice getting to know you like this'. One day those letters will all be found in the archives. So will the memos by which my husband and I communicate too.
Can you believe it?"

The Palace insisted that Charles be at Diana's side after her father died in 1992, although she'd intended to leave Charles and their two boys behind.

"Why are they bothering about him ignoring me now?," she asked. "He's been ignoring me for years already."

Asked if she regretted not becoming Queen, Diana said: "Yes, yes. I could shake hands till the cows come home. And Charles could make serious speeches. But it wasn't to be."

At a private lunch with Tina Brown, editor of the *New Yorker* magazine, and *Vogue* editor Anna Wintour in June 1997, Diana talked of how she had encouraged the Royal Family to employ someone like Labour's Peter Mandelson to improve their image.

"I tried again and again to get them to hire someone like him to give proper advice but they didn't want to hear it," she said. "They kept saying I was manipulative. But what's the alternative – to just sit there and have them make your image for you? Sometimes newspaper editors would write editorials suggesting things they could do. But instead of paying attention one of the private secretaries would ring up and give the editors a rocket."

Shortly before she died, Diana gave her verdict on the rest of the Royal Family. She said that the "antics" of the Duchess of York had not helped the royal cause "and it's a shame for Andrew because he really is the best of the bunch. I mean, people don't know this, but he works really, really hard the country. He does so much and no one pays any attention at all. It's the same with Princess Anne. She works like a dog and nobody cares. And I keep saying to Charles, 'It's no good complaining that people don't care about your work. Until you straighten your head out and get things clear, people just won't give you a break.'"

When Anthony Holden's wife, the novelist Cindy Blake, told Diana that Holden was writing a book about her estrangement from the House of Windsor to be called *The Tarnished Crown*, Diana replied with a giggle: "Perhaps it should be called *The Tanished Tiara*."

When it was published, Holden sent her a copy. She apologised, saying: "I couldn't write to thank you. You do understand why?"

Later he gave her a copy of his biography of Tchaikovsky, telling her not to bother reading it, but just to leave it around for important visitors to see. Within a week, he received a three-page letter, showing that she had read every word.

"It brought tears to my eyes," she said.

Charles

Diana first saw Charles when he came to stay at the Spencers' ancestral seat Althorp in Northampton. Her first impression: "God, what a sad man."

She kept out of the way.

"I remember being a fat, podgy, no make-up, unsmart lady but I made a lot of noise and he liked that," she said. "He was charm himself and when I stood next to him the next day, a 16-year old, for someone like that to show you any attention – I was just so sort of amazed: 'Why would anyone like him be interested in me?'"

They met again at the home of a friend.

"He was all over me again and it was very strange. I thought 'Well, this isn't very cool.' I thought men were supposed not to be so obvious, I thought this was very odd."

But her legendary compassion soon kicked in. "I said: 'You looked so sad when you walked up the aisle at Lord Mountbatten's funeral.' I said: 'It was the most tragic thing I've ever seen. My heart bled for you when I watched. I thought, 'It's wrong, you're lonely – you should be with somebody to look after you.' The next minute he leapt on me practically."

Looking back, she still insisted that Charles had loved her in the early days, particularly when they went on holiday together in the Bahamas.

"Look at those photos. Look how he put his arms around me and gently rubbed suntan oil into me," she said. "How dare anybody say he didn't love me – even if it didn't last?"

Diana soon felt out of place in the world of immense privilege.

"I was always appalled that Prince Charles takes twenty-two pieces of hand luggage with him," she said. "I have four or five.

There were problems with the level of protocol Charles maintained. Diana complained to his valet Stephen Barry: "There I was in a flood of tears, just needing him. And I'm told I have to book an appointment – with my own husband."

It got to the point where Charles and Diana only communicated in writing, via formal memos and Barry was ousted.

Stephen Barry, who had been Prince Charles valet for twelve years, was one of fifty servants who left the royal household after Diana arrived. Afterwards, he wrote two volumes of memoirs, *Royal Service* and *Royal Secrets*, that were published in the United States. British publishers, however, refused to handle them in deference to the palace.

To him are attributed, two quotes from Diana, showing how unhappy she was.

"I don't know what to do, I feel so unhappy here," she reportedly said. "Charles doesn't understand me. He would prefer to be out shooting or stalking or riding or chatting with his mother rather than be with me. Can't he understand that I need him to look after me? I feel he's abandoned me. He just leaves me here all day. I hate it."

Along with Barry, Diana was said to have purged household staff from Charles's bachelor days and those below stairs called her "the boss". But Diana was adamant.

"I just don't sack people," she told the *Daily Mirror*'s royal correspondent James Whitaker. "I am not responsible for any sackings."

When a Sunday newspaper reported how Charles had pointedly ignored her at a concert at Buckingham Palace to celebrate the Queen Mother's ninetieth birthday, she remarked to friends that she found their surprise rather odd. "He ignores me everywhere and has done for a long time. He just dismisses me."

But his lack of feeling for her had begun long before – before they were even married.

"Why does he care more about Camilla than he does about me?" she asked a friend. "I'm the one he's supposed to be marrying, for God's sake."

Diana recognised Camilla as threat from their first encounter. When Charles and Diana were courting, they went to Ludlow Races. Camilla was there too and Diana quickly found herself excluded.

"I felt so vulnerable," she said. "It was clear that I was the outsider in that friendship. Charles was much keener to talk to Camilla than to me. He practically ignored me. I felt that, throughout that whole time, Camilla was simply sizing me up. When Charles finished racing, it was Camilla he ran towards and started talking to. You could tell by the way they were looking at each other that something was going on."

And it was not just Camilla. At a private party she broke away, saying: "I must go and find my husband. As usual, he's surrounded by women."

On one occasion, she told Charles: "You look like a stiff. You embarrass me in front of my friends."

There were other problems with Charles, who she had once called, affectionately, "Hubcap".

"He was in awe of his Mama, intimidated by his father, and I was always the third person in the room. It was never 'Darling, would you like a drink?' it was always 'Mummy, would you like a drink?' 'Granny, would you like a drink?' 'Diana, would you like a drink?' Fine, no problem. But I had to be told that that was

normal because I always thought it was the wife first –
stupid thought!"

When Charles was not away on official duties, he would
go and dine with his mother.

"Why do you do this to me?" Diana complained.
"Why can't we just have a meal alone together for a
change?"

After Charles broken his arm playing polo, he bor-
rowed William's comfortable brass bed at Highgrove.
When his son asked for it back, Charles refused.

"Sometimes I don't know who the baby is in this
family," said Diana.

Her attitude to Highgrove, Charles's country retreat,
changed too. Even as late as 1987, she said: "Prince
Charles loves it and it's my dream home now."

But then Camilla began to act as hostess at dinners
of Charles's closest friends. Going back there then, for
Diana, was "a return to prison".

To compensate for having neglected her, Charles
offered to throw a grand ball to celebrate Diana's thir-
tieth birthday.

"I would hope that my husband would know me
well enough to know that I didn't like that sort of
thing," she said.

Asked by a friend what she planned to mark her tenth

wedding anniversary, Diana said: "What is there to celebrate?"

In 1991 though, she was still defending her marriage. She told most friends that Charles was "the same man today as on my wedding day."

However, that could have meant that she had realised that he had been unfaithful and indifferent to her feelings from the start.

Things got so bad that they lived separate lives, as much as possible. One when Charles arrived home from a private visit to France, Diana immediately left to comfort a grieving friend.

"I'm here for you but I'm also here for me," she told her. "My husband appeared and I just had to fly out and escape."

Asked whether she thought that Charles would ever become king, she said: "Who knows what fate will produce, who knows what circumstances will provoke?"

Was he suited to the role?

"The top job, as I call it, would bring enormous limitations to him, and I don't know whether he could adapt to that."

Towards the end of her life, she gave a more frank assessment of her ex-husband.

"He was born to the wrong job," she said. "Charles is not a leader – he's a follower. He'd have been so happy with a house in Tuscany being a host to artists. He just wasn't cut out for what he got."

Asked if part of Charles's problem was that he had waited for the role of king too long, she replied: "It's up to him to make his role. He could do anything. That's what I have tried to do."

Emerging from the wreckage of her marriage, Diana said: "I had so many dreams as a young girl. I hoped for a husband to look after me, he would be a father figure to me, he would support me, encourage me, say 'well done' or 'that wasn't good enough'. I didn't get any of that. I couldn't believe it, I got none of that, it was role reversal."

Discussing Jonathan Dimbleby's 1994 biography of Prince Charles with the editor of *The Times* Peter Stothard, Diana said: "Do you know that it originally was supposed to contain nothing about our relationship at all? How were readers supposed to think that the [children] came? By immaculate conception?"

"By divine right of kings," Stothard ventured.

"Oh great, by DI-vine right," she said with a giggle. "That's just what did happen."

But Diana knew what came first in her life. She told Charles: "My duty [as a mother] lies above my duty to you."

When the *Sun*'s royal photographer Arthur Edwards

asked Diana whether she intended to go watch Charles play polo, she replied: "No, I'm not going. I hate the game. I don't understand it and I never have. I also hate the sycophants who hang around it. So I'm not going at all this summer. The boys won't be going either. They don't like it and, anyway, it's a waste of quality time."

Before she died, Diana said she wanted to set the record straight "for my boys" on the myth that Charles never loved her.

"That's simply not true," she said. "He did love me. And if anyone ever saw the love letters we wrote to each other they would believe that. It is very upsetting for the boys to hear their father didn't love me. I have to consider their feelings. If they thought Charles hadn't loved me, it would not be good for them."

The Princes

During her first pregnancy, she said, "I cannot tell you how bloody awful it is. They call it morning sickness. But I feel sick all the time."

When the pregnancy was officially announced on 5 November 1981, she said openly: "Some days I feel terrible. Nobody told me I'd feel like this." And she admitted a craving for bacon and tomato sandwiches.

In January 1982, she wrote to Mary Clarke: "I am still feeling and being ill, well into my fourth month and am at total despair and long for the day when I can eventually sit on the loo as to looking over it! Baby Wales is actually due on my twenty-first birthday, but no doubt it will be late."

In early pregnancy, she said: "I hope it's a boy. But we'll have to wait and see."

Before the birth, she told her gynaecologist, Dr. George Pinker: "I shall of course be breastfeeding for as long as possible. I believe it is a very important part of bonding between mother and child."

Then the great moment came.

"I felt the whole country was in labour with me -
enormous relief. But I had actually known William was
going to be a boy, because the scan had shown it, so it
caused no surprise.... Well, everybody was thrilled to
bits. It had been quite a difficult pregnancy – I hadn't
been very well throughout it – so by the time William
arrived it was a great relief because it was all peaceful
again, and I was well for a time."

Postpartum depression came on straight away. She said:
"When I came out of the hospital I could barely put
one foot in front of the other. My stitches were killing
me. It was such a strain to stand there and smile even
for just a few minutes. As soon as the car disappeared
around the comer out of sight of the photographers, I
burst into tears."

Soon she was back to her royal duties and parted from
her baby. She told a woman in the crowd waiting to see
her in Nova Scotia: "I wish I had William with me.
We've been away a few hours, but I miss him very
much. I'm really sorry we couldn't bring him."

When at an early meeting with the press William that
his greatest interest was "exploring wastepaper
baskets," Diana whispered in his ear, approvingly:
"Who's the little superstar, then?"

Her second pregnancy was little better. She said, "I

haven't felt well since day one. I don't think I'm made for the production line."

She decided to renounce any further responsibility, saying: "My husband knows so much about rearing children that I have suggested he has the next one and I'll sit back and give advice."

Nevertheless, at a charity function in 1989, she told a dinner companion: "I want to have three more babies, but I haven't told my husband yet."

Although Diana wanted more children, she knew she had done her duty – providing an heir and spare.

"I came from a family where there were four of us, so we had enormous fun there," she said. "And then William and Harry arrived – fortunately two boys – it would have been a little tricky if it had been two girls – but that in itself brings the responsibilities of bringing them up, William's future being as it is, and Harry like a form of a back-up in that aspect."

When Harry was born, Charles was disappointed that his second child was not a girl. "It's even got rusty hair," he said and left to play polo. Diana later told friends: "Something inside me died."

Later she recalled: "When he was born – it just was bang. Our marriage down the drain. And Charles, all he wanted was a girl. First comment was, 'Oh God it's a boy', second comment, 'Oh no, he's even got red hair!'"

But Diana was sanguine.

"I know we had two boys for a reason. We were the only people in the family to have two boys. The rest of the family had a boy and a girl and we were the first to change and I know fate played a hand there – Harry's a 'back-up' in the nicest possible way. William is going to be in his position much earlier than people think now."

And she was determined to be an exemplary mother.

"I want to bring him and Harry up with security, not to anticipate things because they will be disappointed. I hug my children to death. I get into bed with them at night, hug them and say 'Who loves you most in the whole world?' and they always say 'Mummy'. I always feed them love and affection – it's so important. A mother's arms are so much more loving than anyone else's."

The boys had to be sent away to boarding school though.

"But we have a fabulous time together on their weekends away. I miss them like mad when they're away."

While touring Italy in 1985, Diana told couturier Gianni Versace: "I miss my sons dreadfully. I love them so much, but in different ways. They are so very different. Speaking to them on the phone only makes me miss them more."

On a visit to an orphanage, a thirteen-year-old asked Diana why William wasn't with her. "I didn't bring

William today because he's a little pest. He won't do as he's told and touches everything."

Then, while watching a seventeen-year-old demonstrate break dancing, she told him: "I'll buy you a new pair of trousers if you split those."

Clearly she had experienced this problem at home.

After Fergie and Andrew's wedding in September 1986: "Did you see William? I'm glad he behaved himself because he can be a bit of a prankster. William is just like me, always in trouble, but he'll grow out of it."

Always concerned that her sons would get a grounding in the real world, she said in speech on AIDS: "I am only too aware of the temptation of avoiding harsh reality; not just for myself but for my own children too. Am I doing them a favour if I hide suffering and unpleasantness from them until the last possible minute? The last minutes which I choose for them may be too late. I can only face them with a choice based on what I know. The rest is up to them."

This she felt was particularly important for William, who could one day become king.

"Through learning what I do, and his father to a certain extent, he has got an insight into what's coming his way. He's not hidden upstairs with the governess."

Taking William to a hostel for the homeless, she told friends: "He loves it and that really rattles people."

There were always concerns about her children because

of their unique circumstances.

"I just want my children to be happy and normal," she said. "I will do everything I can to help them achieve these very ordinary feelings."

She also vowed to keep her sons out of the public eye for as long as possible.

"My sons won't be pushed into doing anything public – unlike the Queen and Princess Margaret, who appeared in public at a very early age during the teens," she said. "William and Harry will definitely be broken in gently."

When William played a group of mentally handicapped children at a Christmas party with school friends, Diana said: "I was so thrilled and proud. A lot of adults couldn't handle it."

When William read in the press that Charles had never loved Diana, she reassured him: "When we first married, we loved each other as much as I love you now."

Diana was not happy with Charles parenting. She once told him: "The boys are entitled to happiness and see their father when they need him, not to be told he's running another meeting for the Crisis in Britain League. I need to get away from my royal duties, too; so do you."

On the eve of divorce, Diana reassured journalists: "The boys are both doing very well at school. William is doing well academically and doesn't really like it. He'd prefer to do other things but sticks to his work and is getting on fine."

Parrying criticism for taking her children with her to stay at Fergie's former lover Paddy McNally's villa in the south of France, she said: "They are our children. They are not the possession of the Crown or State."

Asked what she did on the weekends when Charles had custody of their sons, she said: "I stay in town. If I go out, I keep my eyes down or straight ahead. Wherever I go, the press finds ways to spy, you know. Often I visit a hospice."

Two months before she died, Diana said: "All my hopes are on William now. I don't want to push him. Charles suggested that he might go to Hong Kong for the handover, but he said, 'Mummy, must I? I just don't feel ready.' I try to drill into him all the time about the media – the dangers and how he must understand and handle it. I think it's too late for the rest of the family. But William – I think he has it. I think he understands. I'm hoping he'll grow up to be as smart about it as John Kennedy Jnr. I want William to be able to handle things as well as John does."

Of course, the glittering life of John Kennedy Jnr, the first child to be born to a president-elect of the United States and lived in the glare of the media, ended in tragedy when the plane he was flying to the wedding of his cousin, documentary filmmaker Rory Kennedy in Martha's Vineyard, Massachusetts, crashed in Rhodes Island Sound, killing him and his wife, Calvin Klein publicist Carolyn Bessette and her sister Lauren.

After she took William and Harry to see the film *The Devil's Own*, she realised that there would be a storm of criticism in the press, accusing her of sympathising with the IRA.

"I didn't know what it was about when I took them," she said. "We just wanted to see a movie and we picked it out of the paper because William likes Harrison Ford. I issued a statement straight away and I called Charles and left a message. I didn't want him to think I was deliberately making trouble."

In an interview just weeks before she died, Diana said: "My dearest wish is that Charles and I will be able to find a way to do more things together with our sons."

It was not just her own children and Diana cared for.

"What of the children who live with HIV every day? Not because they're necessarily ill themselves, but because their family life includes a mother, father, brother or sister who has the virus. How will we help them come to terms with the loss of the people they love? How will we help them to grieve? How will we help them to feel secure about their future?" she asked. "These children need to feel the same things as other children. To play, to laugh and cry, to make friends, to enjoy the ordinary experiences of childhood. To feel loved and nurtured and included by the world they live in, without the stigma that AIDS continues to attract."

And she had the answer.

"By listening to their needs, really listening, perhaps we can find the best way of helping these children to face their future with greater confidence and hope."

Diana was president of Barnardo's from 1984 to 1996. In 1988, she told the charity's annual general meeting: "I fully realise that for many young people family life is not always a happy experience. They may have been thrown out of their own homes or circumstances may have forced them to leave. Some are homeless, some at risk of drug addiction or prostitution."

In the forward to the *Barnardo's Review* in 1990, she wrote: "During my visits to Barnardo's work I see a very strong commitment to family life. Of course, what constitutes a family today is much broader than in the past. There are single-parent families, permanent foster families and increasingly complicated families resulting from separation, divorce and remarriage. But love, commitment and sharing together are essential ingredients of family life, whatever its form, and it is our task to do all we can to enable children to benefit from it."

Unfortunately her own family life was falling apart at the time.

Diana was stripped of her HRH on her divorce in 1996. With it, she gave up the presidency of Barnardo's after twelve years. In the last issue of the charity's *Review* with her as presidency, she wrote: "Children need every change available to help them along the difficult path to adulthood. A good education, a safe place to live and play, and someone who will listen are all essential ingredients of a decent start in life. Yet many miss out on these seemingly ordinary requirements. Barnardo's continues to work to help make their path a little smoother."

The royal connection with the charity continues though. Queen remains patron of Barnardo's and Camilla, Duchess of Cornwall became its president in 2007.

Praising the work of Relate at the Family of the Year Luncheon in 1990, Diana said: "I know from my own visits to their offices around the country that the experts of Relate have daily contact with the distress which underlies the statistics... Most couples discover and draw on new resources of love and strength. But for many their own resources are not enough."

Sadly Charles was nowhere in evidence.

Presenting the Family of the Year Award, Diana said: "The award is really intended as a tribute to the thousands of family whose daily lives are constructive, loving and unselfish. These are the families who gave the best to each other and to society while quietly coping with a daunting array of pressures."

She put a brave face on it when she attended the ceremony again in 1993, after her separation. Diana remained a patron of Relate until her divorce in 1996.

In 1990, Diana told a Women and Mental Health Seminar: "If we, as a society, continue to disable women by encouraging them to believe they should only do things that are thought to benefit their family, even if these women are 'damaged' in the process, if they feel they never have the right to do anything that is just for themselves, if they feel they must sacrifice everything for their loved ones, even at the cost of their own health, their inner strength and their own self-worth, they will only live in the shadow of others and their mental health will suffer."

This could have been an acute piece of self-diagnosis. Sadly it took years for the healing to begin.

In the foreword to *Once Upon a Christmas* compiled by Ester Rantzen for Childline in 1996, Diana wrote: "Christmas is a time which can be lonely, can be sad, but it can also bring joy, laughter, light, and a time of great blessings to so many."

The year before, she had told a drug-peddler: "I missed my boys at Christmas and the New Year. I spent Christmas alone in Kensington Palace."

At the time, she was visiting the Centrepoint hostel with William and Harry, then thirteen and eleven. The drug-peddler then vowed: "I want nothing more to do with drugs."

Diana concerned about the quality of family life in the

modern world. In conversation with the mother of a child presenting her with flowers at Great Ormond Street Hospital for Sick Children in 1993, she said: "A lot of people watch TV and play so many video games these days they don't really talk to one another… People should be spending time together instead of everybody being glued to the box."

Diana's love of children was conspicuous. "It's amazing how much happiness a small child brings to people," she said.

After watching surgeon Sir Magdi Yacoub perform heart surgery on a seven-year-old boy, flown in from the Cameroon for the life-saving operation in 1996, she told a reporter: "I'm a great lover of children and the fact that a little person can have a second opportunity from my country – I'm very proud to be involved. You gather information much more from a visual contact rather than reading books. So when I stand up and speak about the various subjects, whatever it is, it's more beneficial if I've actually seen it for myself."

Landing in Greece just two weeks before she died, Diana visited the Greek Orthodox church in a small village called Kipazissi with her friend Rosa Monckton. Together they lit candles for their children. "Oh Rosa, I do love my boys," she said.

Family Life

Diana worked hard to hold her marriage together for the sake of her children.

"I think like any marriage – especially when you've had divorced parents like myself – you'd want to try even harder to make it work, and you don't want to fall back into a pattern you've seen happen in your own family," she said. "I desperately wanted it to work, I desperately loved my husband and I wanted to share everything together, and I thought that we were a very good team."

She was all too conscious of problems an unhappy marriage could bring from her experience with her own parents.

"It was a very unhappy childhood, parents were busy sorting themselves out," she said. "I remember seeing my father slap my mother across the face and I was crying on the floor... mummy was crying an awful lot."

It was a lot for a little girl to cope with.

"The whole thing was very unstable," she recalled. "I remember my mother crying. Daddy never spoke to us about it. We could never ask questions. Too many nannies."

The night her parents broke up was "just awful, awful."

Things got little better when her parents divorced when she was seven. The divorce of parent was "a discovery no small child can bear," she said.

Then there was the aftermath.

"Holidays were always grim... two weeks mummy and two weeks daddy."

And there was little support from her elder siblings.

"My sisters always seemed to be leaving me behind."

There were other traumas to deal with. When her mother and father both gave her a new dress to wear at a cousin's wedding, she was caught in a terrible dilemma.

"I can't remember which one I wore," she said, "but I remember being totally traumatised by it because it would show favouritism."

Then there was the problem of being sent away to school.

"There were a lot of tears, because I hated leaving home," she said.

However, it proved a beneficial experience.

"I've built up so much from it, maybe not in the academic world," she said. "I love being outdoors, and I was captain of this and that, and I won endless cups for diving and swimming, which I adore. That's why I really enjoyed it just having lots of friends."

As a child she told her nanny: "I can't wait to grow up and be like my sister Sarah. I can't wait to fall in love and get married and have lots of children. But I'll never marry unless I really love someone. If you're not really sure you love someone you might get divorced. I never want to be divorced."

She was all too well aware of the problems because of the difficulties she had her younger brother had faced.

"Charles and I were horribly different at school because we had divorced parents and nobody else did at that time," she said.

However, in the long run, she recognised that there were some benefits.

"The divorce helped me to relate to anyone else who is upset in their family life."

After her parent's separated, Diana's father won custody of the children as her mother was blamed for the split. Nevertheless, Diana later paid tribute to her capacity to soldier on in the face of adversity.

"I've got what my mother's got," she said. "However bloody you're feeling you can put on the most amazing show of happiness. My mother is an expert on that."

After Diana's parents split, her father, who had by then inherited the title Earl Spencer, married Raine, Countess of Dartmouth, who the children nicknamed

"Acid Raine". When she moved in Diana's older sisters moved out leaving Diana and her thirteen-year-old brother Charles to deal with their stepmother when they came home from boarding school at weekends. The children loathed her.

"I couldn't bear Althorp anymore," Diana said. "A hard Raine was falling."

They also chanted the nursery rhyme "Rain, Rain, Go Away" within earshot.

"I kept thinking and I kept saying to Charles when we're sixteen and when we're eighteen, we'll be able to have our own lives. That's all I could think about. Our own choices."

For Diana, at least, it was not to be.

Open warfare broke out between the Spencer children and their stepmother.

"She's a bully and she just didn't know how to treat individuals," Diana told Peter Settelen. "She [was] just very dismissive. 'Oh Diana, you're so thick," she kept saying. 'You're so silly.' I said, 'I know, but I've got a lot of other things you, you've never found out.' She will one day."

Earl Spencer found himself caught in the middle and, in 1978, suffered a stroke.

"They say, the experts, they say the stroke was brought on by the tension between the four children and a step-mother, which is very true I'm sure," Diana said.

While Diana's father was in hospital, Raine

mounted guard. Diana recalled: "She wouldn't let us see him for about 16 weeks in the hospital."

The final showdown between Diana and her stepmother had to wait until 1989 and took place at the wedding reception of her brother Charles's and his wife Victoria Lockwood where their mother Frances was also a guest.

"My father and stepmother refused to even say hello to my mother," said Diana. "It got me so angry, the behaviour of these grown-ups, that I ploughed in and screamed at both my stepmother and my father. I said it was very bad manners. They were just indulging themselves. And this was Charles' day and Victoria's. Do we have to live in the past every time Mummy walks in the house?"

The anger that Diana had held in check since she was a teenage boiled to the surface.

"My stepmother and I [ended] up having this row," said Diana. "And I pushed her down the stairs, which gave me enormous satisfaction. My father didn't speak to me for six months. I had to go back and say, you know, I love you Daddy, etc., etc., so it was all very difficult."

She found Raine insufferable and could not conceal her emotions.

"I was so angry. I wanted to throttle that stepmother of mine because she brought such grief. She kept saying to me, 'Oh, but Diana, you're so unhappy in your own marriage you're just jealous of daddy's and my relationship.' And jealousy was not high on the agenda. It was behaviour I was after. She said, 'You don't know how much we've suffered because of Frances.' I said, 'Suffering, Raine? You don't know the word. I see suffering of such magnitude in my role that you would never even understand.' I really spat it out at her."

Diana did not mince words.

"I just said, 'We've always hated you. You've ruined our family life. You've done a great job there, Raine? Great job. Made us really unhappy. I hope you're pleased about that.'"

When Earl Spencer died in 1992, Diana and Charles Spencer threw Raine's clothes out of Althorpe. But years later there was a rapprochement when Diana invited Raine to lunch at Kensington Palace.

"I want to thank you for looking after Daddy," she said.

They embraced and Diana cried.

Childhood left other scars on her. When working with voice coach Peter Settelen in 1992, she shared some of the most intimate details of her life, including her struggles with insecurity and low self-esteem that it had left her with.

"I was always told by my family that I was the thick one," she said. "That I was stupid and my brother was the clever one. And I was always so conscious of that. I used to go to the head mistress crying saying I wish I wasn't so stupid."

This stuck with her into adult life. "I was portrayed in the media… as someone, because I hadn't passed any O-levels and taken any A-levels, I was stupid. And I made the grave mistake once of saying to a child I was thick as a plank, in order to ease the child's nervousness, which it did. But that headline went all round the world, and I rather regret saying it."

Although she did not have any academic qualifications, she had a more important one – she was a virgin.

"By the time I got to the top of the school, all my friends had boy friends, but not me," she said. "I knew I had to keep myself very tidy for what was coming. I said to my father when I was thirteen, 'I know I'm going to marry someone in the public eye,' thinking of being an ambassador's wife – not the top one. I always had this thing inside me that I was different. I didn't know why. I couldn't even talk about it, but in my mind it was there."

Later this would play a crucial role in her relationship with Charles. "He'd found the virgin, the sacrificial lamb, and in a way he was obsessed with me."

On her teenage hobbies, she wrote: "My love of my life is dancing, things like tap, modern, ballet and jazz. Also I love singing, even though my voice sounds awful, and watching me dance is like watching an elephant, so no-one does!"

At one time she wanted to be a ballerina, but grew too tall.

"I rather overshot the mark," she said.

Despite the eventually breakdown of her own marriage, she was widely quoted as saying: "Family is the most important thing in the world." And of the circumstances surrounding her own divorce, she said: "What must it be like for a little boy to read that daddy never loved mummy?"

She was particular concerned about the effects on William. "If he thought Charles didn't love me, it wouldn't be good for him – or for Harry," she said.

"Charles did love me when we were married, anyone who saw the love letters we wrote to each other would believe that," she said.

Her concern about the upbringing of William and Harry spilt over into her charity work. As president of Barnardo's she made a televised address in 1988, saying: "As a mother of two small boys, I think we may have to find a secure way of helping our children – to nurture and prepare them to face life as confident and stable adults."

A year earlier, she had told a playgroup in the London borough of Hillingdon: "Harry had some kind of bug and isn't very Well. I did not have a very good night's sleep because he was climbing into my bed. I feel and a bit guilty leaving him to turn up for jobs like this one when one of my own children isn't well."

Another helper said: "It was just like talking to any

other mother."

Despite her glittering image, it was her role as a mother that was most important to her. "I will fight for my children on any level so they can reach their potential as human beings and in their public duties." Elsewhere she said: "…for them to be happy and have peace of mind and carry out their public duties."

But there was more to it. She did not want them isolated from the world in an ivory tower. She told bodyguard Ken Wharfe: "It is so important to me that they grown up not only knowing who they are, but what the world is really like."

She told another friend: "I want the boys to experience what most people already know – that they are growing up in a multi-racial society in which not everyone is rich, has four holidays a year, speaks standard English and has a Range Rover."

More succinctly she said: "I want them to grow up knowing there are poor people as well as palaces."

Good to her word, she took her boys to homeless shelters and hospices. Even during Ascot week, William and Harry were taken to the Refuge night shelter for down-and-outs. William played chess with the inmates while Harry joined in a card school.

"I take them round homelessness projects. I've taken William and Harry to people dying of AIDS – albeit I told them it was cancer, I've taken the children to all sorts of areas where I'm not sure anyone of that age in this family has been before. And they have a knowledge. They may never use it, but it will grow, because knowledge is power.... I want them to have an understanding of people's emotions, people's insecurities, people's distress and people's hopes and dreams."

The other thing she was determined to teach them was: "It's not sissy to show your feelings."

She said elsewhere: "Putting a lid on powerful feelings and emotions cannot be a healthy option."

Perhaps in a reaction to the reserve usually exhibited by other members of the Royal Family, Diana was happy to express her emotions, saying: "As far as I know, crying has yet to kill someone. It does not harm people to cry, or any bystanders. But there seems to be a curious conspiracy in adults to suppress this 'emotion'. People keep trying to stop others from crying as though it will harm them."

Having had the stiff upper lip forced upon, she saw the advantage of letting it all hang out.

"Emotional outburst might be less dramatic or violent if a little steam was occasionally vented harmlessly," she said. "I do not believe that 'emotions' are necessarily nuisances which need to be suppressed or concealed... They are outside signals of inner thoughts. If we try to crush these signals as though they are dirty, an imbalance remains – sometimes for a very long time."

In her campaign for family life, Diana was not alone.

"I wish all the mothers, fathers and children out there realise how much I need them and how much I value their support," she said.

And help came from beyond the grave.

"I'm aware that people I have loved and have died and are in the spirit world look after me."

She was clear about the role of motherhood. "If men had to have babies, they would only ever have one each," she said.

On the other hand: "Men lie less than women, except when they talk about their feelings." This seems to have been a lesson learnt by bitter experience.

In another widely attributed quotation about motherhood, Diana said: "Don't call me an icon. I'm just a mother trying to help." However, Wikiquote have not been able to find precise and reliable source for this, along with the quote about the Queen's dogs: "Oh, no, it's not dogs I don't like – it's corgis. They get the blame for all the farts."

Although the world saw her as a rival to the most glamorous supermodel, it was motherhood that gave her life purpose.

"I live for my sons. I would be lost without them," she said.

She even stayed in Britain after her marriage was over for their sake.

"Any sane person would have left long ago. But I cannot. I have my sons," she told *Le Monde*.

Way back in 1993, the Reverend Tony Lloyd, Executive Director of the Leprosy Mission, had also marvelled at her state of mind.

"I don't know how you stay sane," he said.

"It's prayer, Tony, prayer. It is most important" she replied.

While Charles became a weekend dad, Diana lavished all the attention on her sons that her busy schedule allowed. In 1992, she told a seminar at European Drug Prevention Week: "A child's stability arises mainly from the affection received from his or her parents. With it, children feel increasingly confident to venture out and face the challenges of the outside world… If we can do a proper job of giving our children the affection which nature demands I believe it will help enormously. Hugging has no harmful side effects. If we all play our part in making our children feel valued, the result will be tremendous – there are potential huggers in every household."

Perhaps talking of her own childhood, Diana told the European Society for Child and Adolescent Psychiatry: "Parents sometimes desert families, leaving their children bewildered and bereft with no explanation, let alone the opportunity or encouragement to express their feelings." Just as she had been as a child.

At the opening of Childline in 1988, Diana comforted a girl who felt guilty after she had contacted the charity and, as a result, her father had been jailed for appalling cruelty.

"Have you met any other girls who have been through the same experience?" she asked. "Do you think it might help? I think you might find other young people would make you feel you did exactly the right thing."

During her visit to the charity's headquarters, she listened into calls from desperate children. Afterwards, she told Childline's founder Esther Rantzen: "I'm terribly distressed. What happens to these children? How can we help these children through this? How can we stop it happening?"

"Children are sometimes portrayed as problems to solve and not as souls to love and cherish," she told a drug seminar in 1992. This was interpreted by royal watchers as a swipe at Prince Charles, though she herself later said when she was trying to escape her loveless marriage: "William and Harry are the two problems. But I imagine being a totally fulfilled wife and mother would really be the ultimate happiness, wouldn't it?"

But she insisted to the drug and alcohol charity Turning Point: "Children are not chores, they are part of us. If we gave them the love they deserve, they would not try so hard to attract our attention. In fact the things they do to demand our attention and affection make it hard work. If this empty cavern waiting for affection remains unfilled, it will be filled in some other way. In a stable world this is hard enough, but as the world changes, it is harder and harder to establish this stable platform. But nobody has the time and we are swept further and further away from it by the tides of change."

"I am a great lover of children," she said and she wanted many. "William has brought us such happiness and contentment and consequently I can't wait for masses more."

But she could be strict.

"William and Harry can be little devils sometimes. But when they are, they get a whack where they feel it."

As a dedicated mother, she had words of wisdom to share.

"As a parent I know almost certainly what won't work. Telling children not to do something or trying to frighten them off as all parents know, almost certainly has the opposite effect," she said. "We may have to find a securer way of helping our children – to nurture and prepare them to face life as stable and confident adults."

Diana also brought her own youthful experiences to bear.

"We have all been children, but it is remarkable how quickly childhood and its feelings can seem so foreign to an adult," she said. "We may even as adults try to suppress harmless 'childishness' in ourselves. If we do not help children tackle it, they will carry the burden of imbalance into full-sized adult life. Something might then trigger their disturbance and they may attack others. These others may be their own children."

Bringing up children was not a task she took lightly.

"As parents, teachers, family and friends, we have an obligation to care for our children," she told a conference on eating disorders in 1993. "To encourage and guide, to nourish and nurture, and to listen with love to their needs in ways which clearly show our children that we value them. They in their turn will then learn how to value themselves."

As always, hugs were the answer. She rued: "As countries have become more developed there has been a growing tendency to try to reason affection to our children rather than just be there to provide the support of physical closeness."

Children must be in touch with their feelings. "Unless we teach them how to recognise, share, and understand their emotions, they will lose balance and risk falling off the emotional conveyer belts," she said. "Children who have received the affection they deserve will usually continue to recognise how good it feels, how right it feels, and will create that feeling around them."

There were other things that children had to learn to become rounded human beings.

"There is great scope for children to be taught teamwork, which is directed towards the overall good rather than just beating the opposition," Diana said.

Some problems began before a child was even born. Diana told the European Society for Child and Adolescent Psychiatry in 1991: "Some psychologists believe that problems start in the womb. Morning sickness can affect both mother and child. Cigarettes and alcohol can restrict the child's growth potential; so can anguish or violence around the mother. The outside world they are meant to be joining soon seems less attractive than the warmth of the womb. Often the conflict between parents can distract either parent from meeting the needs of the children; or worse still, the children become pawns in their parents' struggle."

Perhaps, again, this reflected her own situation. Certainly her comments chimed with her own experience of morning sickness.

Her concern for youngsters was anything but a counsel of despair. "It is wonderful to see young people thrive, to see their confidence restored," she said. "I love hearing of their plans for the future and their never-ending optimism."

In 1995, Diana returned to Centrepoint to make the Christmas appeal. This time she said: "Every young person deserves a proper start in life and those who have no family to turn to need to be able to rely on us as a society for the help and encouragement they need. We as part of that society must ensure that young people who are our future are given the chance they deserve."

Speaking as the mother of two inquisitive little boys, she told the annual meeting of the Child Accident Prevention Trust: "I would ask everyone who is buying something for a child this Christmas, however small, to ensure that it is totally safe." She knew how easy it was for accidents to happen.

After the massacre at Dunblane Primary School in 1996, which took the lives of sixteen children and one teacher, Diana wrote to the headmaster, saying: "Like millions of others, I was deeply shocked after hearing of the tragedy that your school has suffered. I know that my words are inadequate but I wanted you to know that everyone who heard the news will silently share your grief. I hope you will find comfort and strength by hearing their prayers and mine.

Tennis ace Andy Murray and his brother and some-time doubles partner Jamie were survivors of the shooting.

But there were limits to Diana's abilities. Interview as president of Barnardo's about her interest in handi-capped children in 1985, Diana said: "I don't know how

I would cope if I had a child who was handicapped or mentally handicapped in some way. So I'm going out there, meeting the children, and I'm learning all the time and trying to understand how they cope."

Then towards the end of her life, she briefly rediscovered the joy of a warm family life.

"Dodi's father has always been like a great uncle to me," she said. "The closeness of our families makes it all the more natural to have my sons in the South of France with me. Dodi and William get on very well. I have rediscovered what a warm family atmosphere can be like."

Divorce

As late as 1991, Diana was still involved in attempts to convince the world that her marriage was doing well. In a story that appeared in *Good Housekeeping*, "Don't worry about me, my marriage is fine. People jump to conclusions so easily."

Soon the tabloids were carrying stories about how much time she spent apart from Charles. She responded: "I sometimes have my friends to lunch if my husband's out. We have people to dinner whenever we can, but my husband goes out to dinners where the wives aren't required, so we can't always find a date to suit both of us."

The British public did not know that the royal marriage was in trouble until the "Squidgygate" tapes emerged. They were recordings of phone conversations between to lovers, who turned out to be Diana and James Gilbey, who repeatedly called her "Squidgy" or "Squidge". They had been touted around Fleet Street for two years, but it was not until they surfaced in the US in 1992 that the *Sun* decided to publish them.

The tape began in mid-conversation, with Gilbey asking: "And so, darling, what other lows today?" Diana replied: "I was very bad at lunch, and I nearly started blubbing. I just felt so sad and empty and thought 'bloody hell, after all I've done for this f**king family...' It's just so desperate. Always being innuendo, the fact that I'm going to do something dramatic because I can't stand the confines of this marriage... He makes my life real torture, I've decided."

The following year, the "Camillagate" tapes came out. These were similar intercepts of mobile phone conversations, indicating that Charles was having an affair with Camilla Parker Bowles.

She later recalled: "The pressure was for us to sort ourselves out in some way. Were we going to stay together or were we going to separate? And the word separation and divorce kept coming up in the media on a daily basis."

That only made the situation more fraught.

"My husband and I had to keep everything together because we didn't want to disappoint the public, and yet obviously there was a lot of anxiety going on within our four walls."

Until then, even though they were seldom seen together, Diana had put a brave face on it, telling a friend: "The truth about our separate lives is very simple. My husband and I get about two thousand invitations to visit different places every six months, so we have to be apart a fair bit. But don't worry about me, my marriage is fine. I have never been happier."

Or so the *Los Angeles Times* reported.

Elsewhere the "friend" reported Diana saying: "…We couldn't possibly get to do many if we did them all altogether so we decide to accept as many as we can separately. This means we get to twice as many places and twice as many people. I don't get the vapours anymore. I think I'm coping much better now."

She also insisted: "Just because I go out without my husband doesn't mean my marriage is on the rocks."

And again: "I know what is going on. I know what people are thinking. Inevitably we are going to be frequently apart. It's the nature of the job. We both do lots of jobs in different directions, but our marriage is very good, thank you very much. We don't see as much of each other as we should."

Clearly Diana knew what she was talking about when she addressed a marriage guidance group in 1992, saying: "I have seen the tears, the anguish, the raw emotions, hurt and pain caused by the split between couples and between parents and children."

But she knew the secrets of survival.

"We've all seen the families of the skilled survivors," she said. "Their strength comes from within and was put there by means of learning how to give and receive affection, without restraint or embarrassment, from their earliest days."

Later that year, she told an anti-drugs seminar: "If the immediate family breaks up, the problems created can still be resolved. But only if the children have been brought up from the very start with the feeling that they were wanted, loved and valued. Then they are better able to cope with such crises and better able to build around them their own affection groups. They'll make friends more easily, find fulfilment in team sports and be better able to build a collective spirit in the workplace or in their community. These are all platforms of mutual affection which help us to survive. Children who have received the affection they deserve will usually continue to recognise how good it feels, how right it feels, and will create that feeling around them. We've all seen the families of the skilled survivors. Their strength comes from within, and was put there by means of learning how to give and receive affection, without restraint or embarrassment, from their earliest days."

Made to the European Drug Prevention Week Media Seminar on 17 November 1992, this is often considered one of Diana's finest speeches and it must have been one of the most difficult to deliver as it was made at a time of great personal turmoil. The official announcement of the royal couple's separation was made just three weeks later. As she spoke she could hardly have avoided having her own situation and children in mind.

Following the announcement of the Wales's separation in December 1992, Diana saw conspiracies everywhere, though she fought back.

"The more they try to damage me, the more they try to undermine me, the more love I feel I have to give out," she said.

According to biographer Penny Junior though, Diana would phone Camilla in the dead of night and say: "I've sent someone to kill you. They're outside in the garden. Look out of the window; can you see them?"

However, in public, Diana was careful not to blame Camilla Parker Bowles, now Duchess of Cornwall, for breaking up her relationship with Prince Charles. But: "There were three of us in this marriage, so it was a bit crowded... the pressure of the media was another factor, so the two together were very difficult."

Once the decision had been made to split, life became very difficult for Diana.

"At the time of the separation I felt deep, profound sadness," she said. "The pressure was intolerable and my job, my work, was being affected. I was constantly tired, exhausted, because the pressure was so cruel."

Although Diana herself admitted adultery, she was taken aback when Prince Charles also confessed to infidelity to Jonathan Dimbleby in his 1994 book *The Prince of Wales: A Biography*. Indeed, she only heard about his confession when it was carried on the evening news. Her first concern was the effect it would have on their children.

"I went to the school and put it to William, particularly, that if you find someone you love in life you must hang on to it and look after it," she said, "and if you were lucky enough to find someone who loved you then one must protect it."

She explained that "although I still loved Papa I couldn't live under the same roof as him, and likewise with him". She did this, she said, "without resentment or anger".

Otherwise: "I think Mr Dimbleby's book was a shock to a lot of people and [a] disappointment."

"I was aware that my husband had renewed his relationship with Mrs Camilla Parker Bowles but wasn't in a position to do anything about it."

This was disingenuous. Diana knew that Charles and Camilla had never parted – and still wasn't in a position to do anything about it.

With Charles, the lawyers, the prime minister and the Queen all involve, Diana grew sick of the wrangling.

"I never wanted a divorce," she said. "No-one seems to understand that. I am now anxious to get all this over with."

Personal matters were being discussed in public and her feelings were sore.

"I would like all the details to be kept private and try to reach a conclusion in a civilised manner," she said. "This is one hell of a week for me. I am totally raw inside."

The media attention was intense and she asked for understanding for herself and her sons from the press.

"I never leave home without feeling acute anxiety and I have felt like a prisoner in my own home," she said.

On the eve of her divorce, Diana said that it had come "sooner and easier than I had anticipated".

"We will continue the arrangement as it is now," she said.

As for reports that she had lost a number of staff over during the negotiations, she said: "There is no problem with my staff. I feel much more in control now and in reality I am only one member of staff short."

After they split, Diana was quoted as saying: "I haven't felt this free since I was nineteen."

Nevertheless: "The fairy tale had come to an end."

After the divorce was finalised, a furious Diana hit back at criticism from Lord Runcie, the Archbishop of Canterbury who had married them, when he branded her "an actress and a schemer". She told friends: "I am appalled by his comments. I thought he was a personal friend and a supporter of my position in the divorce. I will never forgive his treachery."

Charity

On becoming Princess of Wales, Diana said: "I desperately wanted it to work, I desperately loved my husband and I wanted to share everything together, and I thought that we were a very good team."

"I think we had a great deal of interests – we both liked people, both liked country life, both loved children, work in the cancer field, work in hospices," she said.

"I knew what my job was; it was to go out and meet the people and love them," she said. I think that the whole world would agree that she succeeded brilliantly, though it was not so much a job as a vocation.

Gradually alienate from the Royal Family, Diana said: "I found myself being more and more involved with people who were rejected by society – with drug addicts, alcoholism, battered this, battered that – I found an affinity there."

"People think that at the end of the day a man is the only answer. Actually, a fulfilling job is better for me," she said.

The problem was that any man attracted unwarranted press attention.

"Any gentleman that's been past my door, we've instantly been put together in the media and all hell's broken loose," she said. "So that's been very tough on the male friends I've had, and obviously from my point of view."

"I'm not really on my own. I've got wonderful friends, I've got my boys, I've got my work."

According to a confidante, Diana said: "Men need sex, women don't."

After her split from Charles, she said: "I don't know why people think I might fool around. I would remind everyone that I'm still a married woman, apart from being a responsible mother of two."

It was all the fault of the press. On the eve of divorce, she said: "I find it much easier to have a female friend than a friendship with a man. I am always being followed which makes it very difficult."

Her work was particularly fulfilling because of the people she came into contact with.

"Wherever I go I'm privileged to meet so many people who are trying, in so many different ways, to improve the quality of all our lives," she said. "Volunteers and professionals, individuals and groups, from the old to the very young, all bringing people together. All attempting to build, in whatever way they can, a happier community, a better society and a healthier nation. But despite the remarkable work they're doing, there still seems to be a deep concern that something is missing in our society today – a real belief that the community cares!"

And as an individual, Diana was eager to play her part.

"A community is made up of individuals. Every one has their part to play in building a caring community," she said. "Virtually everyone at some point in their lives will need to be cared for by that community. The community is us. If it's denied the nourishment it needs for survival it will fail to flourish. A plant without water will die and so too will the spirit of our community."

Her approach was unlike that of the other royals.

"I remember when I used to sit on hospital beds and hold people's hands, people used to be sort of shocked because they said they'd never seen this before, and to me it was quite a normal thing to do," Diana said. "And when I saw the reassurance that an action like that gave, I did it everywhere, and will always do that."

Sometimes, the words "These people need hope. They also needed encouragement" are added.

Otherwise, the quote is rendered: "I love to hold people's hands when I visit hospitals, even though they are shocked because they haven't experienced anything like it before, but to me it is a normal thing to do."

Even when she was unwell, Diana felt she had to go on

fulfilling the role of the Princess of Wales.

"I felt compelled to perform," she said. "When I say perform, I was compelled to go out and do my engagements and not let people down and support them and love them."

This was its own medicine.

"By being out in public they supported me, although they weren't aware just how much healing they were giving me, and it carried me through."

A naturally shy and insecure person, walking into a room full of people was an ordeal for her – unless she could get her sleeves rolled up.

"I want to walk into a room, be it a hospice for the dying or a hospital for sick children, and feel I am needed," she said. "I want to do, not just to be."

Most of her visiting was done spontaneously and in secret.

Her work with the sick and needy even trumped her love for Dodi Fayed. "Whatever happens to me in this relationship, I will continue to do my work and to help where I am needed," she told her friend Rosa Monckton.

There was another thing she put above Dodi. In a last letter to Rosa, she wrote: "I loved being with you and sharing so many important moments. True friendships are hugely valuable ... we've stuck together through hell and back."

Though being in love with Dodi, she said in a last

phone call to Rosa, was "bliss".

Despite her dedication to good works, Diana was stuck with the image – first of being the fairy-tale princess, then the international celebrity concerned exclusively with shopping and fashion. As a result, she grew used to being patronized by people who met her for the first time. She would tell close friends: "It happens a lot. It's interesting to see people's reactions to me. They have one impression in mind and then, as they talk to me, I can see it changing."

On Diana's desk in Kensington Palace she had a statue of Christ draped with rosaries given to her by the Pope and Mother Theresa. Next to it, her friend Rosa Monckton saw a note in her own hand that read: "You can't comfort the afflicted without afflicting the comfortable."

In a mock interview with voice coach Peter Settelen, Diana asked why doing charity work was so important to her. "Because I've got nothing else to do," she said, laughing.

During a walkabout in Portsmouth in October 1990, when British troops were already deployed for the Gulf War, Diana was asked whether she would be going out to see them.

"It's too early to say when I will go but if the activities carry on much longer, I might well do so," she said.

"I'm very concerned about the morale of the troops and I'm keen to go."

Later she comforted the waiting wives, telling them: "You are not forgotten, especially at Christmas time. There is nothing that I could say which will fill that gap in your lives, and to say that I, along with so many others at home, understand and sympathise with you at this time sounds very inadequate and rather too easy. But it is the least I can do, and I do feel for you, with all my heart."

In Nepal in 1993, she visited a peasant's hut where a single windowless room, thick with smoke, housed a whole family. Leaving she told the press: "I shall never complain again."

Asked why she announced that she was quitting public life in 1993, Diana said: "The pressure was intolerable then, and my job, my work was being affected. I wanted to give 110 per cent to my work, and I could only give 50. I was constantly tired, exhausted, because the pressure was just, it was so cruel.... I owed it to the public to say 'Thank you, I'm disappearing for a bit, but I'll come back.'"

She continued working "underground", but the move did surprise those who were causing her grief.

"I'm a great believer that you should always confuse the enemy," she said.

Who was the enemy? she was asked.

"The enemy was my husband's department,

because I always got more publicity, my work was more, was discussed much more than him."

This angered her husband and his courtiers, but Diana insisted that this was not her fault.

"I wanted to do good things. I was never going to hurt anyone. I was never going to let anyone down," she said.

A few months later, she was at the Serpentine Gallery, chatting with Jeremy Irons, who told her: "I've taken a year off acting."

She replied: "So have I."

"I've had difficulties, as everybody has witnessed over the years, but let's now use the knowledge I've gathered to help other people in distress."

Diana foresaw another important role for herself.

"I'd like to be an ambassador for this country," she said. "I'd like to represent this country abroad. As I have all this media interest, let's not just sit in this country and be battered by it. Let's take them, these people, out to represent this country and the good qualities of it abroad. When I go abroad, we've got sixty to ninety photographers, just from this country, coming with me, so let's use it in a productive way, to help this country."

Diana learnt to deal with the griping of the palace.

"They can't find fault with me when I'm in their

presence. I do as I'm expected, what they say behind my back is none of my business, but I come back here and I know when I turn my light off at night I did my best."

She also complained that were workload ate into her social life.

"I don't want my friends to be hurt and think I've dropped them," she said, "but I haven't got time to sit and gossip, I've got things to do and time is precious."

At one time, she had enjoyed grand events, such as Ascot, but after her divorce she found them frivolous.

"I don't like the glamorous occasions any more," she told friends. "I feel uncomfortable with them. I would much rather be doing something useful."

On leaving public life, Diana apologised, saying: "A year ago, I spoke of my desire to continue with my work unchanged. For the past year I have continued as before. However, life and circumstances alter and I hope you will forgive me if I use this opportunity to share with you my plans for the future, which now indeed have changed."

Everybody needs hugs

"Nothing brings me more happiness than trying to help the most vulnerable people in society. It is a goal and an essential part of my life – a kind of destiny." Diana was firm on the point. "Whoever is in distress can call on me. I will come running wherever they are.

This came from a genuinely egalitarian sensibility.

"I feel close to people, whoever they are. That is why I annoy certain circles," she said. "Because I am much closer to people at the bottom than at the top, the latter do not forgive me."

This was taught to her by her father, the 8th Earl Spencer.

"My father always taught me to treat everyone as an equal. I always have and I am sure that Harry and William are the same," she said.

Earl Spencer had other sound advice that she followed in later life.

"My father said, 'Treat everybody as an individual and never throw your weight around.' I was brought up to look after others."

Recalling her first hospice visit, she told a TV interviewer in 1985: "After I had been round the first ward, I remember it so vividly. I was struck by the calmness of the patients in their beds in confronting their illness. They were so brave about it and made me feel so humble."

"I feel close to people whoever they might be," she told *Le Monde* shortly before she died. "To begin with, we are all the same level, on the same wavelength. That is why I disturb certain people. Because I am closer to people down there than to people higher up they won't forgive me for that. Because I really have close relations with the most humble people."

Diana discovered the power of the hug in July 1991, when she was visiting an AIDS hospice with Barbara Bush.

"I had always wanted to hug people in hospital beds," she said. "This particular man who was so ill started crying when I sat on his bed and he held my hand and I thought 'Diana, do it, just do it', and I gave him an enormous hug and it was just so touching because he clung to me and he cried."

On the other side of the room, she noticed a man crying, while his young lover was dying.

"Wherever I go it's always those like you, sitting in a chair, who have to go through such hell whereas those who accept they are going to die are calm?" she said. "It's wonderful that you're actually by his bed. You'll learn so much from watching your friend."

And it was not just AIDs victims. "It has always been my concern to touch people with leprosy, trying to show in a simple action that they are not reviled, nor are we repulsed," she said. "All people want to be touched."

In a lepers' hospital in Jakarta in 1989, she came across two twelve-year-old suffers playing chess. Via an interpreter he told the two boys: "I play that at home. Who's winning?"

She then bent down and picked up a piece that had rolled under the bed.

At a leprosy hospital in 1989 Diana saw a woman with hardly any fingers making a dress with a treadle sewing-machine. A nurse told Diana, "She came here a leper and is leaving as a Christian seamstress."

Diana went behind a screen to cry, later explaining: "I didn't feel sorry for her, it's a joy. I was happy for her – it's wonderful what has happened to her."

Although many were concerned about the dangers, touching was important to Diana. Asked about it, she said: "Yes, I do touch. I believe that everyone needs that. Placing a hand on a friend's face means making contact, communicating tenderness, establishing one's closeness. It's a gesture which comes naturally to me, which comes from the heart. It isn't premeditated."

The saw "Hugs can do great amounts of good –

especially for children" has also been attributed to Diana, though several other sources had been given the credit.

Elsewhere she said: "Everybody needs hugs."

The efficacy of a hug is a theme that Diana returned to regularly.

"The hug is a simple and highly effective way of sharing concern or showing approval."

"Like crying, a cuddle or hug doesn't hurt, it is cheap, environmentally friendly and needs minimal instruction. It is a simple and highly effective way of sharing concern or showing approval."

"Hugs can do great amounts of good... hugging has no harmful side effects!"

After the IRA bombing in Warrington in 1993, Diana phoned the parents of two boys killed, telling their mother: "I want to hug you."

She had also wanted to visit the scene and pay her respects, but was prevented by palace officials.

When a child rushed up to her in Liverpool in April 1992, in breach of all royal protocol, Diana said: "Of course you can give me a hug."

In 1995, to a twenty-two-year-old blind man who asked whether he could touch her face to find out if she was as beautiful as everyone said she was, she said: "Touch my face. I don't mind at all."

She then knelt down in front of him and put his hand on her face.

Diana had a special affinity with the deaf too. When a five-year-old deaf girl, who was also partially sighted, managed to sign "hello" to her at an awards ceremony for children overcoming handicaps in 1988, Diana touched her chin, the sign for: "Thank you."

When an elderly man who was hard of hearing at a Help the Aged home told her he was ninety-one the deft princess said: "I wouldn't dream of asking your age. I asked where you came from."

For Diana, hospital visits were not a chore, but a fulfilment. "I love it, I can't wait to get into it. It's like a hunger," she said on one occasion. On another: "Anywhere I see suffering that is where I want to be, doing what I can." And another: "Helping people in need is a good and essential part of my life, a kind of destiny."

In this, she was uniquely gifted.

From her work with those with HIV/AIDS and the mentally ill, Diana was quick to see the role that she and others could play.

"Very early on it was realised that they needed a very special kind of support, a very personal kind of attention to help them face their difficulties," she said. "Family and friends were sometimes too close to the problems to be able to really see what was needed, while the experts didn't always have the time to see beyond the symptoms. What was needed was an ally, a 'buddy' to give them one to one attention. Someone who could listen and be there for them."

It was a task she was uniquely suited for – and it was enriching.

"Being a 'buddy' is not easy. But from those I've met the exchange of basic human kindness enriched not just the person being helped but also the person who did the helping. By sharing the successes and the disappointments, a 'buddy' could really make a difference to the lives of those taking their first steps back into the community.

Visiting a sixty-four-year-old retired train driver, dying of cancer in St Joseph's Hospice, Hackney, London, in 1985, she said: "I wouldn't have minded if I'd been a train driver. I've always enjoyed getting up early in the mornings. I do my chores before going out on official engagements."

It had been thought that he had only hours to life. Instead he clung on for another six days.

"I'll always believe that was a special gift from the princess," his widow said.

Explaining her frequent hospital visits in 1995, Diana said: "These people – cancer patients or people with other illnesses – they come out of the operating theatre and come round alone. I try to be there for them. Some will live and some won't – but they all need to be loved while they're here."

Many of her visits were done without the glare of publicity. She made regular visits to two London hospitals and comforted patients who were seriously ill. This brought her solace when her life hit a rocky patch.

However, more publicised visits sometimes invited criticise. When she visited an operating theatre during a heart transplant in Lahore with Imran Khan, she drew flack for wearing full eye make-up.

In her own defence, she said: "If I am to care for people in hospital I really must know every aspect of their treatment and to understand their suffering."

In 1996, she had to postpone a lunch *à deux* with Anthony Holden at Kensington Palace. She apologised, saying: "Magdi Yacoub was performing a heart operation. I had to go."

Holden asked how she would watch such things, saying that he would keel over at the sight of so much blood.

"If I am to care for people in hospital," she said, "I need to know every aspect of the long treatment they have been through."

Diana related something of the experience in a speech at a fund-raising dinner for Sir Magdi Yacoub's Heart Science Research Centre at Harefield Hospital held at Harrod's, courtesy of Dodi's father, the owner of the store Mohamed al Fayed.

"It has been one of my greatest privileges to be

present when a cardio-thoracic operation was carried out," she said. "It was an amazing and enlightening experience. But even more amazing was the effect on the patient. The return of hope on the faces of family and friends is something I will never forget."

Diana herself was the recipient of emergency heart surgery at the Pitié Salpêtrière Hospital in Paris in the early hours of 31 August 1997. But she had suffered massive internal injuries and was beyond saving. She died at 4 am.

In February 1992, Diana visited Mother Teresa's Hospice for the Sick and Dying and met every one of the fifty patients who were close to death. Diana had a natural empathy with people who were close to death or those who had lost a loved one. This was a much publicised event, but she undertook regular visits to hospitals and hospices in the UK and around the world beyond the glare of the cameras.

"I make the trips at least three times a week and spend up to four hours at a time with patients holding their hands and talking to them," she said describing her work with the Royal Brompton Hospital in London. "Some of them will live and some will die, but they all need to be loved while they are here. I try to be there for them", Princess Diana said. "I feel close to people whoever they are – that's why I disturb certain circles. I am much closer to people at the bottom than at the top. I have a real relationship with the most humble people. I've always thought that people need to feel good about themselves and I see my role as offering support to them, to provide some light along the way."

Speaking up for the homeless in 1995, Diana said: "When resources are stretched, those needing help are becoming younger and more vulnerable. Everyone needs to be valued. Everyone has the potential to give something back if only they have the chance. We must ensure young people are given the chance they deserve. It is tragic to see the waste of so many young lives."

This made her the centre of a political storm. Labour spokesman George Foulkes said: "Diana is developing as the people's princess." But then spoilt the compliment by adding: "And she recognises Labour is the people's party."

Meanwhile Tory MPs accused her of breaking rules banning royals from becoming involved in party politics. Sir Patrick Cormack called her a "headstrong and wilful young lady". Fellow MP John Marshall said Di wanted the benefit of belonging to the Royal Family without exercising the concomitant discretion. A third Tory suggested she become a commoner and stand for Labour at the next election.

But Diana was not to be silenced on the matter.

"I have listened to many, many young people whose lives have been blighted by their experiences. Each time I am sad to hear of the abuse and rejection young people have suffered," she said.

Diana returned to the topic the following December, saying: "Homelessness is an experience which isn't confined to the festive season. It is not a problem that miraculously appears on the first day of Christmas and then disappears on the twelfth."

Launching the Christmas appeal for the charity Centrepoint, she said: "If an Englishman's home is his castle, then what happens to that Englishman when he has no home? And if that Englishman is young – perhaps mid-teens, early twenties – what greater risks will confront him? These are the questions which Centrepoint boldly faces each day of the year. And it's doing a tremendous job in helping us understand the real extent and nature of Britain's homeless population. "

"Neither are the homeless made up of twenty and thirty-year-olds who have had their chance at life and failed miserably. The age of homeless youngsters is coming down. Children as young as eleven called on Centrepoint this year."

Having heard about the Osteopathic Centre for Children in London from Rosa Monckton, mother of a Down's syndrome daughter, Diana paid a secret visit. When director Stewart Korth told her their treatment was revolutionary, Di laughed and replied: "Well, you've got the right person, then – I'm the ultimate rebel."

In her first public engagement after the summer holidays in 1997, Diana was to have launched the £2 million Sweet Pea appeal for the centre. As it was, her place at to be taken by six-year-old Laura Stanford, who suffered from cerebral palsy.

"I am doing a job for Diana," she said, "and it makes me feel very special."

The following year the centre was awarded £1 million from Diana's memorial fund.

At a fund-raiser in Sydney for the cardiac specialist Dr Victor Chang, who was murdered in 1991, Diana praised his work and said: "It has been said that for evil to triumph, good men must do nothing."

The original – "The only thing necessary for the triumph of evil is for good men to do nothing" – is generally attributed to the eighteenth-century parliamentarian Edmund Burke.

The speech was made at the Victor Chang Cardiac Research Institute in 1996.

"Tonight, we give heartfelt thanks that a good man, Dr Victor Chang, did a great deal and that we can all be thankful as we look forward to the future," she added.

Diana turned her attention to cancer in Chicago in 1996, saying: "The dreaded C word – it seems to strike from nowhere, destroying lives almost at will, leaving devastation in its wake. But the advances that have been made are quite staggering. It may not always be possible to provide the complete solution to a patient's predicament but does that mean we should give up? Sometimes we may only be able to provide support and counsel. Does that mean we have failed? I think not."

Attending the symposium on breast cancer in her capacity as president of the Royal Marsden Hospital, she said: "There are few subjects more likely to raise anxiety and fear than cancer. It seems to strike out of nowhere, destroying lives at will, leaving devastation in its wake. While few of us may be able to pioneer a new form of surgery or test a new drug, we can support those who do. We can raise money for research and work in other ways to ensure that the fight against this disease continues to press ahead."

Visiting a cancer patient at Northwestern Memorial Hospital in Chicago, Diana put her arms around the man's weeping wife and said: 'It must be very difficult for the whole family, but you have very good support. You support each other."

That same year, she gave a speech at a gala in the National Building Museum in Washington, DC in aid of the Nina Hyde Centre for Breast Cancer Research at Georgetown University, where she said: "It is a word of just six letters but has the power to strike panic, fear and anxiety into the hearts of us all… From where I sit, looking in from the outside, I sense that the fight has begun."

Diana was equally sympathetic in 1986 when an eighty-two-year-old woman who was dying of cancer said that she wanted to see the daffodils bloom again.

"Try to keep your spirits up," said Diana.

Diana had special affinity for the Royal Marsden hospital and remained president after her divorce and the loss of her title. In the foreword of its 1997 information brochure, she wrote: "You only have to spend a short time at the Royal Marsden Hospital to feel its special atmosphere of care, confidence and cheerful efficiency. The methods of treatment pioneered by this hospital and the caring skills of its staff have enabled thousands of people to face cancer with hope and have laid to rest the myths and stigma that have for so long surrounded the disease and its treatment. Sadly, all the goodwill in the world cannot meet the continuing demands for better facilities, more sophisticated technology and new developments, which is why we should all bring to this hospital the support it deserves."

The Royal Marsden was one of the major beneficiaries of the auction of her dresses held at Christies, New York, two months before she died.

In a speech for Turning Point in 1990 she said: "It takes professionalism to convince a doubting public that it should accept back into its midst many of those diagnosed as psychotics, neurotics and other sufferers who Victorian communities decided should be kept out of sight in the safety of mental institutions."

Diana also railed against society's intolerance of those suffering from mental illness – those who "the circle of ignorance, fear, and prejudice spins to condemn.

Casting them in the role of the untouchables, the people to be avoided at all costs. Disabling them, for being different. Denying them their God given right to be included, to be part of their community. Denying them their right to live without fear of ridicule, hate and exclusion."

Diana found comfort herself making these visits.

"I respected very much the honesty I found on that level. In hospices, for instance, when people are dying, they're much more open and vulnerable and much more real than other people," she said. "I appreciated that."

She also admired that quality in Prince Charles when he admitted being unfaithful with Camilla.

"I was pretty devastated myself," she said. "But then I admired the honesty, because it takes a lot to do… to be honest about a relationship with someone else, in his position – that's quite something."

Anger

Diana also turned her energies into fighting addiction. "Nature has a funny way of sending us what we most resist," she said. "None of us can remain smugly immune from addiction, whether it is chocolate, cigarettes, alcohol, drugs, or even work."

"Addiction can strike any who suffer distress in their personal or professional lives," she said. "Alcohol and drugs do not respect age, sex, class or occupation, and the line between recreational use and creeping addiction is perilously thin."

"The grim realities of drug abuse, you would think, ought to provide all the evidence needed to dissuade the most sceptical teenager. But the message so often seems to be lost unless this evidence is presented in ways which stop young people in their tracks."

In 1986, Diana was the first of many celebrities to sign the "Say No to Drugs" pledge organised by Westminster City Council.

"Drug abuse is becoming more and more widespread," she said. "Addiction knows no class barriers. I'm extremely concerned as any mother would be."

She was right to be worried. Later Harry took to smoking marijuana. At Eton he was as "Hash Harry" or "His Royal High-ness" and, at one time, his drunken antics were legend. However, GCHQ had been keeping his acquaintances under surveillance and MI5 leaked the information to Charles. William also volunteered the information that Tom Parker Bowles had been arrested for the possession of marijuana and ecstasy. He was later caught using cocaine.

In a confrontation with his father, Harry confessed everything, but he thought it unfair that he was blamed when William, who he felt was equally culpable, got off scot-free. Nevertheless it was Harry that Charles sent a drink-and-drug rehabilitation centre in south London that he had officially opened the previous year. The visit seems to have done its job, temporarily at least, scaring Harry off drink and drugs.

Although alcohol and drugs were enough of a menace in themselves, they brought with them fresh dangers.

"I am appalled at the dangers young people face on the streets and how vulnerable they are to exploitation," Diana said. "Sixteen and seventeen year olds who resort to begging, or worse, prostitution, to get money to eat. Young people whose physical and mental health has been severely damaged by life on the streets. Young people who take drugs to provide some escape from the hardship they face. Young people who have been attacked and abused on the streets and face the indifferent stares of passers-by who have no idea how brave they are or how much they have suffered. It is truly tragic to see the total waste of so many young lives – of so much potential."

She added: "Those who have no family to turn to need to be able to rely on us as a society for the help and encouragement they need."

As with her other concerns, Diana showed a genuine understanding of the problem.

"As in any other illness, the approach to addiction has two components – prevention and cure," she said. "The clues to prevention lie in the understanding of what drives people to addiction or into a state where they are vulnerable to addiction. They all agree that it does not really improve their lives, so why do they do it? Mood changing substances do not exactly last very long. When I have asked addicts why they became addicted the most common reason is anger. Anger at their parents, anger at their schools, anger at their communities. In fact, anger at life in general. But why the anger? It seems to stem from their feelings of instability in a changing world. In many cases they have felt deprived of affection as children and the stability which this provides. So they've sought this affection in other ways such as from possessions, on the grounds that if they're surrounded by material goods they must be doing well and be acceptable. Or they may try to cushion themselves behind mood changing drugs. They are all looking for a firm emotional base."

"Very often, it is in the home that the climate for addiction is created," Diana told a symposium organised by Turning Point, a charity which helps addiction sufferers, in 1989. "And equally often. it is in the home that its worst consequences are felt. A stable domestic background, where the simple duties of family life are shared and understood, can do much to strengthen those tempted to find a refuge in drink or drugs."

"It is sometimes argued that addicts bring their problems on themselves. But I have noticed that those who have first hand knowledge of what these problems are, seem less inclined to pass judgment."

"Those who imagine that drug and alcohol problems mainly affect the less fortunate members of our community would be quite wrong. On the contrary, addiction can strike anyone who suffers stress in a personal or professional life."

Diana returned to the question of drugs – or "mother's little helpers" – in a speech on "Women and Mental Health" in 1993. In it, she asked: "Isn't it normal not to be able to cope all the time? Isn't it normal for women as well as men to feel frustrated with life? Isn't it normal to feel angry and want to change a situation that is hurting?"

She went on to say: "Those women who have taken on the heavy burden of attending to others need also to be attended. Not just for their own sake but for the good of us all. Health and happiness taken at the cost of others' pain and suffering cannot be acceptable.

Women have a right to their own peace of mind."

Three times the number of tranquilizers, sleeping pills and anti-depressants were given to women as to men. "For those who find the courage tentatively to ask for help, 'the pill for every ill' is most often administered," Diana warned. "These 'mother's little helpers' have left a legacy of millions of women doomed to a life of dependence from which there is very little escape."

In another appeal for women, Diana said: "Each person is born with very individual qualities and potential. We as a society owe it to women to create a truly supportive environment in which they too can grow and move forward. But if we are to help the quiet private desperate lives lived behind closed doors by so many women, they need to know for certain they are not alone – that real support and understanding is there for them."

At the Brampton Hospital in London in 1986, she was shown slides of diseased lungs in 1986 and told doctors: "These should be shown on television so everyone could see the damage smoking does."

Four years later the manager of a hotel in Bath told her that he had set aside a third of the rooms for non-smoker.

"I'm delighted," she said. "Smoking is an unhealthy habit. I welcome any step forward in making people more aware of the importance of good health."

She even had "no smoking" signs in Kensington Palace. Unfortunately, without a mother to guide him, Harry became a Marlboro man.

In 1992, at a Turning Point clinic, Diana told one anorexia sufferer and former drug addict: "Don't be harsh on yourself."

These were words that she eventually applied to herself.

AIDS

Diana's work with AIDS victims was groundbreaking. She was one of the first high-profile celebrities to be seen touching a sufferer way back in 1987 and as credit with helping to remove the stigma formerly associated with the disease.

"HIV does not make people dangerous to know," she said. "So you can shake their hands and give them a hug: Heaven knows they need it."

Diana was particularly conscious of this. She said: "For me, one of the particularly sad things about my visits has been to find out how much stigma people with AIDS and HIV still suffer and how much they feel they have to deal with prejudice as well as their physical problems."

When courtiers suggested that ministering to AIDS victims was unsuitable for a young princess, Diana said: "No one else will help these people and I feel I must do something."

She had a warning for those who wanted to ignore the problem: "We cannot afford to think of HIV and

AIDS as someone else's problem and put it to the back of our minds. If we do, we risk turning what is, in the end, just another life-threatening illness into a plague which will create fear and suspicion in place goodwill and humanity."

In a speech "Women and Children with AIDS" given in Edinburgh in September 1993, Diana said: "Some sections of the media would have us believe that the dark shadow of AIDS is fading away. The predicted explosion has failed to happen and retreated back to those who've so often been condemned or ignored...."

Clearly, she meant gay people.

"...The truth is that most people infected by HIV are heterosexual and the disease is spreading, throughout the world, at a staggering rate."

As a mother, Diana identified closely with mothers and children who had AIDS.

"A mother with HIV or Aids doesn't give up the responsibility of caring for her children easily. Often she is the sole parent, the wage earner, the provider of food, the organiser of daily life, the nurse to other sick members of the family, including her own children. Relentless demands continue to be placed on her, at a time when her own health and strength are falling away."

She spoke from the heart when she said: "A mother with HIV carries the grief and guilt that she probably won't see her healthy children through to independence. If she has passed on HIV to one of her children, she will have to witness their illness while trying to make something of their short life. Worrying as to what will happen to them if she dies first."

Her own children were just eleven and eight at the time.

"Trying to plan for her surviving children's futures won't be an easy task!" she said. "At what stage should she give up her role as a parent? Who can she rely on to take care of them? Where can she find the right kind of support to decide what is best for them? How can she be sure that her family history and traditions won't be lost?"

Did these thoughts flash through her mind in her dying moments?

Women with AIDS faced particular concerns she told the Second Conference on HIV in Children and Mothers at the Heriot-Watt University, Edinburgh, in 1993: "Despite information about AIDS being available for nearly ten years, these women still face harassment, job loss, isolation, even physical aggression, if their family secret gets out... Relentless demands continue to be placed on her when her own health and strength are falling away. As well as the physical drain, a mother with HIV carries the grief and guilt that she probably won't see her children through to independence."

On top of everything else, AIDS sufferers had to

endure social ostracism, something Diana sought, by example, to overcome.

"The biggest fear of the mothers I've met with HIV or AIDS is not their disease," she said. "They've learnt to live with their disease, especially, as for much of the time they are feeling well! No, what terrifies them most, is other people! For despite information about Aids being available now for nearly ten years, these women still face harassment, job loss, isolation, even physical aggression, if their family secret gets out."

This posed a very real dilemma, one similar to the one she had faced when her marriage began to fail.

"How then is it possible for them to decide the moment to explain to their children what is happening in their lives? Do they tell the neighbours? Do they tell their children's school? Is there anyone they can truly trust or is it safer and wiser to struggle on alone?"

"Yet these mothers don't ask for sympathy. Their need is for understanding. To be allowed to live a full and active life. To be given the support to love and care for their children, for as long as they can, without carrying the added burden of our ignorance and fear."

In 1994, Diana invited a young mother dying of AIDS contracted through a blood transfusion on a reception at Kensington Palace. The woman had already lost one child to the disease and Diana had visited her and her sick child in hospital. After the reception, Diana wrote her a note, saying: "It meant so much to me that you were there last night. I am thinking of you."

Diana had seen the effects HIV and AIDS was having on a trip to Zimbabwe where the disease had been allowed to spread unchecked.

"I saw for myself the very personal tragedies whole families were suffering," she said. "The damage it was doing to their communities, to the country as a whole, both socially and economically, was devastating."

This was no counsel of despair.

"The support these families were given by those around them was a lesson for us all," she said. "They were being treated with compassion and respect, by their friends and neighbours, for what they were having to go through. And were still accepted as an important part of their community, not as outcasts to be ignored.

While the number of AIDS sufferers in the UK was comparatively small, Diana made a heartfelt plea: "If we continue to believe that AIDS is someone else's problem, we too, could so easily be facing the same devastating destruction of our nation's way of life that is already happening in other parts of the world."

She called for more understanding and for people to "be just a little more aware and just a little less embarrassed about how the virus is transmitted, even when we don't really see ourselves at risk. In that way, perhaps, we may play a small part in helping to protect a person we love from becoming infected with HIV."

Diana was a beacon of hope. "For those mothers and children already living under the dark shadow of AIDS we need to help them back into the light," she said. "To reassure them. To respect and support their needs. And maybe, we will learn from them, how to live our own life more fully, for however long it is."

Bulimia

After William's birth, Diana said: "I was unwell with post-natal depression, which no one ever discusses, you have to read about it afterwards, and that in itself was a bit of a difficult time. You'd wake up in the morning feeling you didn't want to get out of bed, you felt misunderstood, and just very, very low in yourself."

"People were – when I say people I mean friends, on my husband's side – were indicating that I was again unstable, sick, and should be put in a home of some sort in order to get better. I was almost an embarrassment," she said. "It gave everybody a wonderful new label, 'Diana's unstable and Diana's mentally unbalanced.' And, unfortunately, that seems to have stuck on and off over the years.

"When no one listens to you, or you feel no one's listening to you, all sorts of things start to happen," she said. "You have so much pain inside yourself that you try and hurt yourself on the outside because you want help."

But this was easily dismissed by others.

"People see it as crying wolf, or attention-seeking, and they think because you're in the media all the time you've got enough attention."

Unable to cope with the pressures of being the Princess of Wales, she cut her arms and legs. Curiously though, it helped her in her work.

"I work in environments now where I see women doing similar things and I'm able to understand completely where they're coming from," she said.

Diana had bulimia for a number of years. She called it her "secret disease".

"You inflict it upon yourself because your self-esteem is at a low ebb, and you don't think you're worthy or valuable," she explained. "You fill your stomach up four or five times a day – it gives you a feeling of comfort. It's like having a pair of arms around you."

"Then you're disgusted at the bloatedness of your stomach, and then you bring it all up again."

"When you have bulimia you're very ashamed of yourself and you hate yourself," she said, "and people think you're wasting food, so you don't discuss it with people."

And while anorexics visibly shrink, bulimics stay the same so the condition is easy to hide.

"I'd come home feeling pretty empty, because my engagements at that time would be to do with people dying, people very sick, people's marriage problems," she said, "and it would be very difficult to know how to comfort myself having been comforting lots of other people, so it would be a regular pattern to jump into the fridge."

The real problem was her failing marriage. But the bulimia gave out the wrong signals.

"People were using my bulimia as a coat on a hanger," she said. "They decided that was the problem: Diana was unstable."

As a result, Diana was put on high doses of Valium.

"All the analysts and psychiatrists you could ever dream of came plodding in trying to sort me out, they were telling me 'pills'! That was going to keep them happy – they could go to bed at night and sleep, knowing the Princess of Wales wasn't going to stab anyone."

In 1992, she explained to Peter Settlelen: "The odd thing was when I was bulimic I wasn't angry because. The anger, I thought, was coming out that way. And it always felt better after I'd been sick to get rid of the anger. And I'd be very passive afterwards. Very quiet." "Rampant bulimia, if you can have rampant bulimia, and just a feeling of being no good at anything and being useless and hopeless and failed in every direction… with a husband who loved someone else."

Diana began to address the problem in a speech about "Eating Disorders" in April 1993.

"I have it, on very good authority, that the quest for perfection our society demands can leave the individual gasping for breath at every turn," she said. The authority was her own.

Acknowledged as one of the most beautiful women in the world, she continued: "This pressure inevitably extends into the way we look. And of course, many would like to believe that eating disorders are merely an expression of female vanity – not being able to get into a size ten dress and the consequent frustrations."

"From the beginning of time the human race has had a deep and powerful relationship with food," she said. "Eating food has always been about survival, but also about caring and nurturing the ones we love. However, with the added pressures of modern life, it has now become an expression of how we feel about ourselves and how we want others to feel about us."

The result was distress and low self-esteem.

"Eating disorders, whether it be anorexia or bulimia, show how an individual can turn the nourishment of the body into a painful attack on themselves, and they have at the core a far deeper problem than mere vanity."

"Eating disorders are on the increase at a disturbing rate, affecting a growing number of men and women and a growing number of children, too."

She had been to Great Ormond Street Hospital for Sick Children and met some young people who were suffering from eating disorders.

"With the help of some very dedicated staff, they and their parents, were bravely learning to face together the deeper problems, which had been expressed through their disease," she said. "With time and patience and a considerable amount of specialist support, many of these young people will get well. They and their families will learn to become whole again. Sadly, for others it will all be too late.'

"From early childhood many had felt they were expected to be perfect, but didn't feel they had the right to express their true feelings to those around them – feelings of guilt of self revulsion and low personal esteem. Creating in them a compulsion to 'dissolve like an asprin' and disappear," she said.

The illness she called a "shameful friend… an expression of how you feel about yourself and the life you are living".

"By focussing their energies on controlling their bodies they have found a refuge from having to face the more painful issues at the centre of their lives. A way of coping, albeit destructively and pointlessly, but a way of coping with a situation they were finding unbearable – and express of how they felt about themselves and the life they were living."

And she made a broad appeal for more support and advice, saying: "With greater awareness and more information, these people, who are locked into a spiral of secret despair, can be reached before the disease takes over their lives. The longer it is before help reaches them, the greater the demand on limited resources and the less likely it is they will fully recover."

Diana said she was certain that the ultimate solution lies within the individual, though some needed help professionals, family and friends,

"People suffering from Eating Disorders can find a better way of coping with their lives," she said. "By learning to deal with their problems directly in a safe and supportive environment."

It was a question of "giving back to these people their self esteem. To show them how to overcome their difficulties and re-direct their energies towards a healthier, happier life."

Eventually in November 1993, Diana went public with her condition, stunning the audience at a London charity event with an unscheduled announcement.

"Ladies and gentlemen," she said. "I was supposed to have my head down the loo for most of the day. I'm supposed to be dragged off the minute I leave here by men in white coats. If it's all right with you, I thought I might postpone my nervous breakdown."

Just four months before she died, Diana explained how she had beaten bulimia.

"I go to the gym three times a week to get rid of my pent up anger and aggression now," she said. "I'm not obsessed with it."

But the spectre still haunted her.

"I could go back to bulimia again but it's not an option. I'm over it and I've been like that for two years. I beat it by myself, for me."

Landmines

In her campaign against the use of landmines, Diana became political. In 1997, she said of incoming Labour government under Tony Blair: "It's going to do terrific work... Their position has always been absolutely clear."

By contrast John Major's outgoing Conservative government was "absolutely hopeless". Conservative minister Earl Howe retaliated, dismissing her as a "loose cannon".

Shocked by the criticism, she replies: "Who says I am a loose cannon? I'm not a political figure, neither do I want to be one."

She went on to insist: "I'm a humanitarian, not a political figure... All I'm trying to do is help. I am trying to highlight a problem that is going on all around the world."

Diana believed that the smear campaign was master-minded by her old foe Armed Forces minister Nicholas Soames, a close friend of Prince Charles, but shrugged it off.

"I saw the row at Westminster as merely a distraction which meant things went off the rails for five minutes and went back on again," she said. "It's not helpful things like that but it does happen when a campaign is entwined in a political issue. I understand that."

"Over the years I've had to learn to rise above this sort of thing. The irony is that it's been useful to me in giving me a strength I did not think I had," she said. "That's not to say that the criticism hasn't hurt me. It has. But it has given me the strength to continue along the path I've chosen."

About the new prime minister Tony Blair she said: "I think at last I will have someone who will know how to use me. He's told me he wants me to go on some missions. I'd really, really like to go to China. I'm very good at sorting people's heads out."

In January 1997, Diana explained how she had become involved in the anti-landmine campaign, saying: "A lot of information started to arrive on my desk and the pictures were so horrific that I felt if I could be part of a team to raise the profile around the world, it would help."

As a result, Diana travelled to Angola where fifteen million landmines had been left behind in a devastating civil war. On the trip, she said in an interview: "You read the statistics, but actually going into the centres and seeing them struggling to gain a life again after they have had something ripped off by something on the ground – it is shocking. I have seen some horrifying things over the years, but I have learned to cope with it because each person is an individual, each person needs a bit of love. You don't think about yourself."

The head of the Red Cross Federation in Luanda, Angola, told her: "If you really want to see the effects of mines, look around you."

Diana replied: "I looked into their eyes and saw it all."

Diana told the *Sun*: "I have never been to anywhere like this before. I was open minded about it but I am surprised by the level of injuries I have seen. I found it very humbling. The number of amputees is quite shocking. Going into the centres and seeing them struggle to gain a life again after they have had something ripped off by something on the ground – it is shocking."

She had learnt to live with the shock and horror of it all.

"I have seen some horrifying things over the years but I have learned to cope with it because each person is an individual," she said. "Each person needs a bit of love. You don't think about yourself."

But the experience took its toll. Asked if the harrowing things she had seen had an effect on her, Diana said: "Always, always you take it home with you."

Diana relished the new role she had found for herself.

"I have had hands-on experience before. This has been slightly different. I have had more contact with the people – there's been less formality," she said. "It's the type of format I have been looking for, for some time and I'm very happy with the way it has gone. I have had both ends of the spectrum, some of it official but most of it informal. You have to have one with the other. But I have always wanted to do visits like this."

She drew succour from the experience.

"My lasting impression is of the hope generated in this country - they have so many problems," she said. "And of people like the Red Cross and all the other organisations who are doing wonders."

Diana told the Red Cross that the most poignant memory of her January 1997 mission to the Angolan minefields was the sight of a seven-year-old Helena Ussoua whose intestines had been blown out.

"She was very, very poorly," said Diana. "Just looking at her and wondering what was going, on inside her head and heart was very disturbing, yet she was just one of the statistics. It was very touching."

Kept alive by a saline drip, the child, who was still conscious, did not know who Diana was and asked: "Is she an angel?"

Diana described the scene as "so poignant, so very poignant", saying that Helena's face would haunt her for the rest of her life.

"Nothing can prepare you for the appalling pain and suffering anti-personnel mines can inflict on innocent children and civilians," she said. "I hope to make more visits like this in the future. There are so many countries that need help in some way and there are millions of landmines lying dormant. Someone's got to do something."

Diana wrote and narrated the script of BBC's *Heart of The Matter Special: Diary of A Princess* about her trip. In it there was a clip of her sitting on the little girl's bed, saying: "When you see children like that it brings it all to the surface. That was very traumatic, as a mother, to witness. We must end the use of these lethal weapons."

Le Monde said that she had been compared to Brigitte Bardot, who took to animal activism and rightwing politics after retiring from the cinema. Another critic said: "The subject is much too complicated for her bird-brain."

Again once admitting to being "as thick as a plank" came back to haunt her. Although the political controversy was a distraction, this cloud had a silver lining.

"The row ruined a day's work but it increased the media coverage tenfold," she said.

She grew increasingly frustrated by politicians. "What's to discuss, when people are being blown up?" she said.

"I can't tell you how much my landmine project means to me. And yet I am criticised. I cannot win."

At a one-day seminar called "Responding to Landmines: A Modern Tragedy and its Solutions" co-hosted by the Mines Advisory Group and the Landmine Survivors Network on 12 June 1997, Diana said: "The world is too little away of the waste of life, limb and land which anti-personnel mines are causing among some of the poorest people on earth. Indeed, until my journey to Angola early this year, I was largely unaware of it too. Indeed, until my journey to Angola early this year I was largely unaware of it too. For the mine is a stealthy killer. Long after the conflict is ended, its innocent victims die or are wounded singly, in countries of which we hear little. Their lonely fate is never reported."

She repeated the message a speech at a red cross gala in Washington, D.C., on 17 June 1997 saying: "Having seen for myself the devastation that anti-personnel mines cause, I am committed to supporting in whatever way I can the international campaign to outlaw these dreadful weapons."

She stressed the necessity of a ban because of the magnitude of the problem.

"Achieving a global ban is one step because mines are being laid at a rate of two million a year but being removed at a rate of only a hundred-thousand a year. But helping mine victims themselves is equally important particularly as the one hundred ten million mines currently being made world wide will kill and maim for many years to come."

Afterwards she visited a landmine victim in Bethesda Naval Hospital. While working for the Organization of American States removing landmines along the Honduran–Nicaraguan border, Brazilian Rul Xavier DaSilva had stepped on one and lost a leg and a foot.

Diana took the matter so seriously that risk further criticism by taking to the pages of the *Daily Mirror* on 6 August 1997 with a thousand-word article on the subject. In it, she said: "Some people chose to interpret my visit as a political statement. But it was not. I am not a political figure. My interests are humanitarian. That is why I felt drawn to this human tragedy. That is why I wanted to play my part in working towards a worldwide ban on these weapons."

She talked of the victims she visited and their injuries: "When you look at the mangled bodies, some of them children, you marvel at their survival."

And she drew attention to the "chronic shortage of medicine, of pain killers, even of anaesthetics. Surgeons constantly engaged in amputating shattered limbs never have all the facilities we would expect to see here. So the human pain is beyond imagining."

Two days later she flew to Bosnia as part of her anti-landmine campaign. Visiting Sarajavo, she said: "I have seen lots of poverty before but I have never seen such devastation."

On 12 August 1997, she wrote to Jerry White, co-founder of the Landmines Survivors Network: "I was enormously impressed by the genuineness of your approach to the survivors and their families to sustain their morale and to help them maintain their self-esteem. Their tragic stories are a desperately sad reflection of man's inhumanity to man. The victims I have met and their senselessly inflicted injuries have stiffened my resolve to ensure that their needs for care and support are not overlooked in the search for an agreement to outlaw landmines."

The Media

As first Diana found the press intrusion intolerable, particularly when journalists took a flat across the road from the one she shared with three flatmates and spied on them with binoculars.

"I cried like a baby to the four walls," she said. "I just couldn't cope with it. I cried because I got no support from the Palace press office. They just said, "You're on your own."

Charles was no help either. He was more concerned about the press outside Camilla's house in Gloucestershire.

"I asked him, 'How many press are out there?" He said, "At least four." I thought, 'My God, there's 34 here!'"

Nevertheless Diana learnt to put a brave face on it. In a Q&A session with Grania Forbes of the Press Association in July 1981, she said: "I've been extremely touched by everyone's enthusiasm and affection. It has taken a bit of getting used to the cameras but it is wonderful to see people's enthusiastic reaction; it is most rewarding and gives me a tremendous boost. The Prince of Wales has made everything far easier for me and it is very good to be able to do things together publicly. I miss the immediate company of my flatmates. I'm enormously grateful to the many people helping so well with all the wedding arrangements and very much looking forward to visiting Wales and getting to know it better as part of my duties as future Princess of Wales."

In her first days of public life, on a crowded shopping street in Mayfair, someone called out: "Di!"

Diana said: "Please don't call me that – I've never been called Di. I really don't like it."

However, to the redtops she would be Di for the rest of her life.

On her first trip abroad as Princess of Wales, to Australia, she complained: "The whole world was focusing on me every day. I was in the front of the papers. I thought that this was just so appalling, I hadn't done something specific like climb Everest or done something wonderful like that."

She went to her lady-in-waiting and cried he eyes out, saying: "Anne, I've got to go home, I can't cope with this."

Even after the birth of Prince William, Diana could not understand the media's obsession with her.

"As far as I was concerned I was a fat, chubby, 21-year-old, and I couldn't understand the level of interest," she said.

Although judged to be one of the most beautiful women in the world, she was reportedly not happy with her looks.

'I don't like this awful mole I have above my top lip," she was quoted saying. "I think my legs below the knees are far too thin. I would love a fuller figure, particularly up top." And "I hate my nose. It's so large. One day I'm going to have my conk done."

In 1991, Diana lamented: "When we first got married, we were everyone's idea of the world's most perfect couple. Now they say we're leading separate lives. The next thing I'll read in some newspaper is that I've got a black lover. No, to make matters worse, I'll have a black Catholic lover."

The pressure was unrelenting. Towards the end of her life, she lamented: "The press is ferocious – it forgives nothing. It only hunts for mistakes. Every intention is twisted, every gesture criticised. I believe that abroad it is different. I'm welcomed with kindness. I'm taken for what I am, without prior judgement, without looking for blunders. In Britain it's the opposite. And I believe that in my position anyone sane would have left a long time ago."

"The pressure on us both as a couple with the media was phenomenal, and misunderstood by a great many people. We'd be going round Australia, for instance, and all you could hear was 'oh, she's on the other side'. Now, if you're a man, like my husband a proud man, you mind about that if you hear it every day for four weeks. And you feel low about it, instead of feeling happy and sharing it. "

Never had anyone been under such scrutiny. "Here was a situation which hadn't ever happened before in history, in the sense that the media were everywhere, and here was a fairy story that everybody wanted to work," she said.

But then the public had been sold the fairy tale, something that no normal relationship could stand up to.

"We were a newly-married couple, so obviously we had those pressures too, and we had the media, who were completely fascinated by everything we did," she said. "It was difficult to share that load, because I was the one who was always pitched out front, whether it was my clothes, what I said, what my hair was doing – which was a pretty dull subject, actually, and it's been exhausted over the years – when actually what we wanted to be, what we wanted supported was our work, and as a team."

At the start, they were part of the same package. She said: "We got out the same car, we shook the same hand… my husband did the speeches, I did the hand-shaking… so basically we were a married couple doing the same job, which is very difficult for anyone, and more so if you've got all the attention on you."

Eventually the attention of the media came between them.

"My husband decided that we do separate engagements, which was a bit sad for me, because I quite liked the company," she said. "But, there again, I didn't have the choice."

The media also intruded into their private life, making more of a rift.

"Because again the media was very interested about our set-up, inverted commas," she said, "when we went abroad we had separate apartments, albeit we were on the same floor, so of course that was leaked, and that caused complications. But Charles and I had our duty to perform, and that was paramount.... We were a very good team in public, albeit what was going on in private. We both made mistakes."

The consequences were inevitable. "We had unique pressures put upon us, and we both tried our hardest to cover them up, but obviously it wasn't to be," she said.

Diana surprised group of photographers who chanced across her outside a Klosters café. She pointed to the outsize medal on her jacket, jokingly: "I have awarded it to myself for services to my country because no-one else will."

Perhaps the subtext was her alienation from the rest of the Royal Family who are conspicuous for their range of beribboned uniforms.

But Diana knew how life with the paparazzi was going to be even before she was married. Announcing her engagement on 25 February 1981, the *New York Times* reported: "During the ordeal of pursuit to which Fleet Street reporters have subjected her in recent months, she has shown good humour and patience, although once, surprised by photographers at the wheel of her red Mini Metro, she burst into tears. 'I know it's just a job they have to do, but sometimes I do wish they wouldn't.'"

The constant media attention took its toll. "I had a very bad time with the press – they literally haunted and hunted me. I haven't felt well since day one. I don't think I'm made for the production line."

Withdrawing from public duties in December 1993, she said: "When I started my public life 12 years ago, I understood that the media might be interested in what I did. I realized then that their attention would inevitably focus on both our private and public lives. But I was not aware of how overwhelming that attention would become; nor the extent to which it would affect both my public duties and my personal life, in a manner that has been hard to bear."

She added: "I hope you can find it in your hearts to understand and give me the time and space that has been lacking in recent years." It was a *cri de coeur*. At last, she hoped to be free of media harassment. In fact, it only fed the appetite of the paparazzi.

On a skiing trip the following year, she complained of the pack of paparazzi that had taken to the slopes, telling James Whitaker, royal correspondent of the *Daily Mirror*: "When I see them around all the time it is like being raped."

Diana also said it was "like a rape" when pictures of her sunbathing topless on the Costa del Sol were being touted for £1 million by a Spanish photographic agency in 1994.

Diana felt that the media had turned her into a commodity.

"You see yourself as a good product that sits on the shelf and sells well, and people make a lot of money out of you," she said.

However, she granted that the media had proved useful to her in her humanitarian campaigns.

"Being constantly in the public eye gives me a special responsibility, particularly that of using the impact of photos to get a message across, to promote an important cause, to defend certain values," she said. "If I had to define my role I would use the word messenger. I pay great attention to people and I always remember them. Every visit, every meeting is special."

She also turned to the media to help with her anti-addiction campaign. After all they owed her.

"Like it or not I have been quite a provider for the

media and now I'm asking for your help to reduce the suffering caused by drugs," she said. "The help which you can give could be direct or indirect. Direct help for those already caught in the drugs trap; indirect for those who are not yet caught... Direct help also includes highlighting what works in helping addicts – the individual successes, the groups, the communities. In other words, helping to acknowledge the challenges they have overcome; and also some of their solutions. From the media point of view these successes do make great stories. The process of passing though addiction can reveal a soul of great depth. Moreover, a watching addict is much more likely to gain hope from someone who has been there and who also understands the feelings which led them there. More than from a knowledgeable official who has read up on it. Direct help can also include fundraising to help the support groups."

Diana was not just the victim of the press. Sometimes she struck back with criticism of her own.

"The media could emphasise the value of having had a good game in which one team happened to win, rather than focus entirely on the so-called victor as though victory is the only thing that matters," she said.

By 1995, when she had separated from Charles and cut down on her public duties, she found that she was even more in demand.

"I understand that when I get out the car I'm being photographed, but actually it's now when I go out of my door," she complained. "I never know where a lens is going to be. A normal day would be followed by four cars; a normal day would be to come back to my car and find six freelance photographers jumping around me."

To the paparazzi, she was still a commodity.

"They've decided that I'm still a product – after fifteen, sixteen years, that sells well – and they all shout at me, telling me that: 'Oh, come on, Di, look up. If you give us a picture I can get my children to a better school.'"

"I've never encouraged the media," she said. "There was a relationship which worked before, but now I can't tolerate it because it's become abusive and it's harassment. But I don't want to be seen to be indulging in self-pity. I'm not. I understand they have a job to do."

Diana's last interview was given to *Le Monde*. The article was headline "The Big-hearted Princess" and part of a series where celebrities talked about their favourite portrait. Taken in February 1996, the photograph showed her hugging a blind child with a brain tumour in a hospital in Lahore.

"The child died soon afterwards... I will never forget him," she said. "If I had the choice, it's in these kind of surroundings that I would prefer to be photographed. I touch people. I think that everyone needs that, whatever their age. Placing a hand on a friend's face means making contact, communicating tenderness, establishing one's closeness. It's a gesture which comes naturally to me, which comes from the heart. It isn't premeditated."

She realised that with all the attention they attracted, they were inevitably riding for a fall.

"The most daunting aspect was the media attention, because my husband and I, we were told when we got engaged that the media would go quietly, and it didn't," she said. "And then when we were married they said it would go quietly and it didn't; and then it started to focus very much on me, and I seemed to be on the front of a newspaper every single day, which is an isolating experience, and the higher the media put you, place you, is the bigger the drop. And I was very aware of that."

In an appeal for privacy, she told the press: "You in the media are all part of a powerful industry. That power can be used destructively or constructively!"

In an effort to get them to mend their ways, she said: "I would welcome the establishment of a prize for the most successful media idea that demonstrates the power of collective spirit and effort!"

Taking her last holiday on board Mohamed al-Fayed's yacht moored at St Tropez, Diana told the *Daily Mirror*'s royal correspondent James Whitaker: "You are going to get a big surprise with the next thing I do."

"I've opened up. My life is changing. This is only the beginning," she said.

Diana told Whitaker that William and Harry

believed that only by living abroad could she escape the media's constant intrusion into her life and preserve her sanity.

"My boys are urging me continually to leave the country," she said. "They say it is the only way. Maybe that's what I should do. They want me to live abroad. I sit in London all the time and I am abused and followed wherever I go. Now I am being forced to move from here."

She had wanted to go to Barbuda, but the media attention there would have been impossible too.

"William is distressed. I was hoping to keep this visit all covered up and quiet. You expect me to sit in Kensington Palace? I don't have the boys in August. And I just want a summer holiday with my boys."

Indicating the photographers, she told Whitaker: "I am talking to you because I can't to them. I don't speak their language. I just want a holiday with my boys. William gets really freaked out."

She was also quick to defend the Harrod's owner.

"Mr Fayed was my father's best friend," she said. "I have known him for ten years. Anyway, to be strictly correct, I am here with his wife."

She later rued: "There is nothing personal in my life any more. Press covers every step I take."

Lord Stevens report into the death of Princess Diana, published in December 2006, nearly a decade after the fatal crash, finally revealed what her last words were.

Gendarme Sebastien Dorzee arrived at the scene at 12.30. Two minutes later, paramedic Xavier Gourmelon arrived at took over her care. He told the enquiry that the princess had become agitated. Seeing Dodi Fayed dying, she said: "My God. What's happened?"

After that, her speech became incoherent. She lapsed into a coma and was rushed to hospital where she died without recovering consciousness. Photographs taken by the paramedics were later destroyed by the French authorities.

At a fund-raising dinner for breast cancer research at the National Building Museum in Washington, DC, in 1996, Diana had quoted the words of Australian poet Adam Lindsay Gordon:

Life is mostly froth and bubble
Two things stand like stone
Kindness in another's trouble
Courage in your own.

These lines could have been her epitaph.

Having spend much of her life comforting the dying and bereaved, Diana had said: "Death doesn't frighten me."

Ever since, Diana's death has been the subject of conspiracy theories. She too subscribed.

"One day I'm going up in a helicopter and it'll just blow up," she reportedly confided to a friend. "MI5 will do away with me."